FLIPPING HOUSES

Learn About Flipping Houses for Fast Real Estate Profit

(How Are So Many People Getting Rich Flipping Houses)

Mark Lefebre

Published By John Kembrey

Mark Lefebre

All Rights Reserved

Flipping Houses: Learn About Flipping Houses for Fast Real Estate Profit (How Are So Many People Getting Rich Flipping Houses)

ISBN 978-1-77485-250-7

All rights reserved. No part of this guide may be reproduced in any form without permission in writing from the publisher except in the case of brief quotations embodied in critical articles or reviews.

Legal & Disclaimer

The information contained in this book is not designed to replace or take the place of any form of medicine or professional medical advice. The information in this book has been provided for educational and entertainment purposes only.

The information contained in this book has been compiled from sources deemed reliable, and it is accurate to the best of the Author's knowledge; however, the Author cannot guarantee its accuracy and validity and cannot be held liable for any errors or omissions. Changes are periodically made to this book. You must consult your doctor or get professional medical advice before using any of the suggested remedies, techniques, or information in this book.

Upon using the information contained in this book, you agree to hold harmless the Author from and against any damages, costs, and expenses, including any legal fees potentially resulting from the application of any of the information provided by this guide. This disclaimer applies to any damages or injury caused by the use and application, whether directly or indirectly, of any advice or information presented, whether for breach of contract, tort, negligence, personal injury, criminal intent, or under any other cause of action.

You agree to accept all risks of using the information presented inside this book. You need to consult a professional medical practitioner in order to ensure you are both able and healthy enough to participate in this program.

Table of Contents

Introduction 1

Chapter 1: What Is House Flipping? 4

Chapter 2: The Financial Perspectives And Understanding Your Market 16

Chapter 3: Kinds Of Home Repairs That Aren't Valued 28

Chapter 4: Finding Great Deals 34

Chapter 5: Five Items That Will Make Your Flip Flop 50

Chapter 6: How Is The Best Place To Look For Houses That Are Suitable To Flip 62

Chapter 7: What Do Earn 6 Figures In Real Estate? 67

Chapter 8: Creating An Action Plan 73

Chapter 9: Tips To Consider Prior To Purchasing An Investment Property 80

Chapter 10: What To Purchase 87

Chapter 11: Significant And Not So Important Fixes That Need To Be Made 109

Chapter 12: Aesthetic Update Option .. 117

Chapter 13: Tax On House Flipping Consequences 123

Chapter 14: Property Criteria Comfortable Underground Sales Price 127

Chapter 15: Funds In Flipping 135

Chapter 16: Unimaginable Value Of Immovable Property 151

Chapter 17: Final Thoughts 172

Conclusion 185

Introduction

Maybe you've seen several shows that focus on flipping houses or perhaps you know someone who is interested in this and makes an enormous amount of cash from just a small number of transactions per year. Perhaps you're fed up with the monotony of working 9-5 and would like to retire early and be into the game. But, you're in a bind as to where to start and how to do the process.

In reality, many people have been in the same position. The bad news is that a lot of have failed before they achieved success, while certain people were able to achieve success in a way that others could not. What could they have done differently? What can you do to be one of them?

The good news is that you have already taken the first important step in the right direction by purchasing this book. This book you'll learn everything you have to know about the house flipping industry. Additionally, you will learn how to choose the right property to flip as well being able to get the funding needed to flip your home.

This book will guide you through the steps of determining whether you have the right skills and resources to buy or renovate properties. It will also demonstrate how to estimate your income prior to making your first offer to purchase the property. We will discuss these subjects as well as many others.

The book is categorised into different sections that will assist you achieve your home flipping goals. They include:

Part 1 - Mindset

Section 2 - Expanding your understanding

Section 3 - Choosing the right house

4. Section 4 - - Viewing and purchasing

Section 5 - Earning a little money

Section 6 - Selling the product

I cannot guarantee that you won't encounter bumps along the way. Being a successful home flipper is not without many challenges. However, I am certain that once you've finished the book, you will have a deep understanding of everything it takes being a successful home flipper. If you make use of all the information in this book it will allow you to start a profitable side-business from the beginning and earn a steady income.

It has been a blast researching the book. I truly hope that you be able to comprehend it as you read.

Let's start our journey towards a successful house flipping business.

Chapter 1: What Is House Flipping?

House flipping typically means that after the repairs or upgrades are completed, the home is bought and then resold to earn profits. What is "quickly" differs. You can define it as being within 6 months.

In the end, it's about buying a house which is likely to be profitable and will soon be resold. It is a common practice in the booming property market specifically for real estate professionals.

It is a profit-making strategy in which investors purchase real estate for less and renovate the real estate so that it can be sold at higher rates. If the market for housing is stable, this can be an extremely profitable method.

Older homes and mortgages are the most popular property used for flipping homes due to investors being able to buy these homes for very little which can increase the potential profit. In certain instances contractors are hired to make real estate improvements However, experienced house flippers could complete the job themselves.

Market dealers often use the same method but they also keep sellers and buyers in stock to allow more efficient transactions. But this has not been viewed as a good thing. But middlemen never get good news.

If the house price decreases, those who are able to sell their property are in danger of losing money on their investment , as the gain could be enormous when house prices rise.

FLOOR FLIPPING in 2019

The process of relocating your house might seem easy, but it's the process is not as simple as it seems. Let's turn it into a the reality. House flips can be fantasies and catastrophes.

If done correctly If done correctly, flipping houses can be an investment of a lifetime. In a short period of time you can do an intelligent renovation and then sell your house for much higher than the price you bought it for.

But, flips of homes can be to the wrong place when done in the wrong manner. I've heard of a horror story that flips the house. It appears to be a home with a rocking foundation and a roof that leaks, which appears to be attractive. When you're done with your day, turning the home over might not earn the homeowner money. In reality, it costs you thousands.

If you choose to sell the property over, you definitely would not like to lose the money. You'd like to make smart investment decisions and reap the rewards. If you do not have the most up-to-date knowledge of the real estate market in the area You can't flip the house around.

It is the only method to tell whether a house is truly a bargain is to know the value of comparable homes within the vicinity.

You'll have all the time you need to obtain a real-estate license in order to gain access to the multiple listing services in the area. This offers two advantages. You are able to access both sales and price offers and can identify it when it's available and help you locate the best deals.

It must be bought at WELL in the current market Never ignore this process. If you think of the final sale price of an item as a retail price the price you pay will be considered to be a wholesale cost. The difference will provide plenty of benefits and the ability to fund renovations of your property.

If you are buying a house that reverses You shouldn't make a purchase by relying on your emotions (I truly love this home). Your success is largely on your numbers and you have to be able to accept the numbers.

Earning LEVEL In FLIPPING HOUSES

The company that collects real estate data ATTOM revealed that the average earnings of House flipping US during the 2nd quarter of 2018, was 65,520.

In contrast, ATTOM considers all housing that is sold or bought within a calendar year (with as well as not real estate) however, it only considers the purchase price, minus the sale price. The flippers who are experienced will inform you that they're not the only crucial numbers.

A single flip of a house is approximately $30,000 and is a fair estimate for the majority of home flippers. The figures decrease for flips with low prices and rise for higher-end flips.

The amount of money you can earn from flips and corrections is contingent on the worth of the deal and the house. You can set a minimum goal for each fix and turn a an income of at least $25,000.

There are numerous risks involved with fixing or turning your home over. It is not advisable to sell if there isn't a possibility of earning at least $25,000. The more expensive the home is, the higher risk and expenses, and the less you will earn more.

You will also be able to figure out the amount of money you will need for the job you want to do. If you are looking for homes that need significant renovations, you'll need to make more than $30,000. If a home just requires carpet and painting it is simple and quick, and you is able to take a tiny profit.

The hazard of a homicide flying

If HOUSE FLIPS are a good investment The tax rate will be higher.

"Flipping" is an expression used to describe selling a home prior to closing it, usually by making someone pay for the assignment of the purchase contract. But, the majority of people employ this term more frequently to mean buying a property and then selling it for a higher cost. You could earn some money in the event that it is successful, however the tipping process is costly.

Risk of losing money

One of the main negatives of flipping a house is that it's not always go as planned. If you aren't able to sell your purchase contract and you lose your deposit when you pull out or be unable to purchase an unplanned property.

Purchase, rehab and sell flips may cause losses If the rehabilitation rate is higher than anticipated, or in the event that the market moves downwards or in the event that the buyer is not attracted by the property.

OPPORTUNITY COST

If you can make a profit from flips, you will likely get a good deal in the first time you contract an agreement to purchase a home. If you decide to flip it, you will earn the capital and profit, however you have to invest that capital.

The property that you buy as rental properties can produce solid monthly cash flow. In the opposite, it is a missed chance to earn that continuous income stream.

FLIPPING PART-TIME FOR HOUSE

There is an excellent possibility of a part-time flipping a house. In reality, there is no distinction between full-time flipping house or part-time.

Reasons to FLIP HOUSES Part-Time

Are you looking for extra income? Flipping a couple of houses per year can be an ideal way to earn an extra revenue on the side.

A busy schedule or a lack of time - Someone who has an active schedule may choose to sell a couple of homes rather than flipping nothing even.

Have Fun with Your Current Full-Time Job Some flippers opt to work part-time in flipping because they work full time in a job that they enjoy or love and they'd like to stay in.

Beginning to Get Started Like I said, working part-time to flip houses is an excellent opportunity to begin the industry.

A lack of resources to flip houses takes a lot capital and resources, and many people have only enough capital or resources to flip a single house at a time.

PRECAUTIONS WHEN FLIPPING HOUSES APART TIME

While flipping houses part-time is possible and could provide many benefits, there are some risks and traps to be wary of when you are flipping houses part-time.

The first thing to keep in mind is that part-time house flipping doesn't mean that there isn't any work involved to flip a house.

Flipping houses requires an enormous amount of time and effort and simply because you decide to work part-time in flipping does not mean that there is less effort or work required.

The most significant distinction between part-time and full-time house flipping isn't how much work required but how long the job is completed.

One of the major issues and obstacles when flipping houses in part-time is the risk of shortages in market knowledge that can result in bad decisions and eventual loss when flipping houses.

Be aware that simply because it's been months since you last sold an apartment does not mean that the market for real estate isn't frozen.

The real market for real estate and the prices of housing remain in a constantly changing and fluctuation. Therefore, when you are flipping houses for part-time, it's essential to be informed and up-to the latest information regarding the local market for real estate.

Tips for FIPPING HOUSES On the Side

Set a timetable and stick to it. when you're flipping houses for a part-time basis, it's easy to drift off-track or let a whole week slip without completing anything. Although you may be moving in a slower manner, it's important to keep your house flip going forward.

Be realistic about your expectations Do not expect full-time outcomes with part time work. If you intend to do house flips part-time, do not expect to earn an enormous amount. House flipping is an excellent source of income however, just like all businesses, you only get the amount you put into.

Keep up-to-date with current developments in the Real Estate Market - Just that you decide to flip houses on a part-time basis does not mean you don't need to be aware of the same data that a full-time home flipper has.

Be vigilant about Contractors - If you're working part-time on flips and working with contractors or subcontractors, do not assume that everything is getting done while you are away. It's crucial to keep an eye on your property every day or at least once a week to ensure that the work is being completed at the right time and in the right manner.

Think about hiring a Project Manager When you're a part-time home flipper, you may not always be present on the job site. If your budget permits for one, you may think about hiring a manager for your project who will work in your instead.

Regularly check the property If you're flipping houses part time, make sure you check on the flips you have made regularly. If a property is empty, things could be a problem, such as vandalism or leaks in the water which is why it's essential to inspect the property regularly to ensure that the property is safe and safe.

Always keep an eye out for the Next Flip If you're flipping for part-time, it's easy to let yourself slip in your search for the next flip. Be aware that whether you flip houses in part or full-time getting inventory on hand is essential to any profitable house flipping business.

Chapter 2: The Financial Perspectives And Understanding Your Market

One of the primary factors you must consider is the financial. There is no escaping the fact that you're investing money. This section will cover a variety of financial factors that must be considered prior to making an offer to purchase a home. It is essential to get this aspect correct because if you are out of cash and you are unable to pay for it, you may end up having a home on your hands for a lengthy period of time and losing money instead of earning it.

Day 3: How much can you spend?

In the initial three days, it is important to choose the amount you are able to spend. This doesn't only pertain to the property. It can also mean the remodeling. The total amount you spend will depend on your personal circumstances however, you must be aware that you need to set an upper limit on the amount you can afford for your home as well as renovations. If you're thinking of using borrowed funds the process becomes more complicated. If you borrow money, it will cost you more due to the fact that for every day it is due you'll have to pay interest. If you truly are trying to be honest regarding your financial situation, the interest payment should be taken into consideration. In the event that you face difficulties selling your home. Are you able to make the monthly payments? If you're looking to take out $100,000, it would cost you as much as $460 per month for thirty years. This means that each month that the loan is not paid, you could take $460 out of the profit, which isn't the most efficient way to proceed.

It is possible that you however you have accumulated some funds, and typically those who have been able to inherit funds or gained by selling an enormous house in order to move to a smaller house have funds left in the pot they invest in property.

The calculations for your finances should include the costs of owning the property. This means that you will have to pay for charges for utilities to the property until you've closed on it. If you are calculating the price of a home that you want to purchase, it is important to keep in mind the costs of running the house once you've purchased it , as well as any interest that you might have to pay in financing. Be aware that the loan you take out could also come with a penalty for late payment which is why it's an issue to consider when you are trying to earn cash. Be aware that banks can be charged to arrange loans. The amount over and above the value of the home as well as the expense of renovating is known as a contingency plan and is crucial to the investment. The contingency fund can also be used the possibility of unexpected renovations which you might find necessary due to the areas of your house not being conforming to the standards.

If you decide to finance your venture with loans, you should arrange it to know precisely how much you are able to spend. Make enough time to review your finances, and then think about what you want to accomplish. Make a trip to your bank. Determine the amount of money available and then be prepared to tackle the challenge of becoming an investor in property.

The issue with homes that are cheap is that they are snapped up swiftly, which is why you shouldn't play with them. You must be aware of your maximum limit to ensure that if a property is in excess of that and there's not much possibility of negotiation, you are able to walk away and not waste your time.

Day 4: Learning About the Market

If you make a bet on an area you're not familiar with, you could be losing money.

When flipping a house, the research that you conduct will help you make a more secure investment. The property might appear inexpensive on the surface however, what will determine the price compared to other homes is

* Location of the house

* Areas where the house is

* Suitability to current market conditions

• Equity on the property

Why are these things important so significantly? The truth is that home prices differ from one part of a town to the next depending on a variety of factors. If you're used to living in a high-priced section of town, but suddenly discover a home that's cheap elsewhere, that doesn't mean it's expensive in the eyes of those who live in the region. It's the reason you need to do some research. You must compare like to like in the same geographic area to determine if the price is as inexpensive as you think.

Check it against other homes for sale and inquire from the local real estate agents if the market in this particular region is thriving in the present. Conversations with friends can reveal many different details. An excellent indicator that a region is growing is when you can see commercial builders' vehicles taking away old homes, which typically means that renovations are underway and is an indication that a specific region is likely to be getting better. This is an excellent point to consider for you since an area that has been improved generates interest. The day could involve buying local newspapers, and conducting a lot of research but it's worth it.

The location plays significant roles in value, therefore don't fall into believing that a home is cheap because it's located in a low cost region. If the area isn't expensive that means the list cost you can afford to offer for the house should reflect the area. Many property owners fall short. They believe that the product that they possess will be worth much more money than what it is. They then lose money. Take a look at other homes in the same neighborhood and gain a clear understanding of the prices and examine houses that match to the one you're contemplating buying. You can get more value for price in lower region, but you'll need to ensure that your offer is an excellent value for buyers seeking houses in that region. They'll also be aware of the typical costs.

Day 5 - Learning About Potential Properties

With so many bargains to be found on the market it's easy to get overwhelmed by your ideas about purchasing. But, you must have to be aware of the market and specifically properties within the location you're considering. The home you purchase should be in line with the other properties. If it's not up to the mark today, it will at some point when you've revamped it. There are a variety of factors to be considered that will be covered in the book to come however at present, you should be aware of how your home compares to other properties for sale in the same region. Do you have a nice landscaping? Are schools close by? Are they near universities? Could it be a good option for business-minded people?

Through studying your market you will have an idea about the kind of client you'll be dealing with. In the event of a mishap, you could find that you own the property in the near future. As an example, converting the house into a three bedrooms family home situated in the middle of a college city might not be the most wise choice. In the same way, if you convert the house into executive homes located situated in a family-oriented residential zone, it's unlikely you'll attract top executives. This is why having a good understanding of the neighborhood is crucial. Explore the area take a break and speak to people , and discover the kind of customers you could draw, as it gives the potential buyer an understanding of what price you could offer for the property after all the work is completed.

Property Brothers Property Brothers are particularly good in finding homes that they can improve for their cash However, they are aware of exactly what they are looking for. Also, you must be aware of what the house is hidden, and this requires some time and experience.

Day 6 - Learning About Your Potential Workforce

If you are in the region in which you purchase a house it is necessary to look inside some of the houses available for sale. This will give the buyer an understanding of the standards which people will be comparing your home to. If you're not skilled in electrical installation or plumbing and electrical installation, you must have an electrician as well as a plumber on your team that is able to perform at a fair price. If you are an investor in property on a frequent basis, you could benefit from the incentive that if a tradesman offers you an offer of a discount, you might be able to work with him. Find out the names of your local tradesmen and how effective they are and also determining their availability and their hourly rate. A successful homeowner will work with the same workers all the time and will come to rely on them.

They are needed by tradesmen, and the earlier you locate the team of people who you can count on the more reliable. Other trades you might require to learn about are carpenters, roofers dry wall installation contractors , and the ones who put up insulation. Be aware that when trying to turn a house around do not be sloppy however, you must try to save money wherever you can. If you or a non-skilled worker are able to save time by having the space ready to be used by drilling holes into walls where they are required and saving money. The various decorating tasks you can perform yourself will reduce the total costs, and even though you'll have to find materials, you'll be in a position to create an expense list of the things you buy and ensure that you stay within your budget.

Knowing about the potential suppliers is also crucial. If you've watched Property Brothers, they don't purchase items from random stores. They know which places to take their clients to purchase the various items they use in their homes. These include:

* Tile

* Flooring

* Baseboards

* Crown moldings

* Kitchen cabinetry

* Kitchen worktops

* Kitchen Island furniture

* Fireplaces

If you work with the same suppliers regularly There will be discounts for you. It's important to consider which suppliers you choose to cut hundreds of dollars off your investment. Let the suppliers know you're a business owner and are likely to utilize regularly and you'll be amazed at by how they are compelled to offer you a greater discount. If they are only offering an introductory discount, consider alternatives, but don't be low-cost. It isn't a good idea for your home to be fitted with fixtures and fittings that aren't worth the price since it will deter prospective buyers who need top-quality houses. It's not worth cutting corners. If you do, you ruin your reputation, and immediately attract those who are hoping to buy your home at a cheaper cost since they will have to fix what you have done wrong.

If you can provide them with their dream homes and sell it to the most suitable people, you could make money and all you need is a little foresight as well as a ability to negotiate with your suppliers to accomplish this.

Chapter 3: Kinds Of Home Repairs

That Aren't Valued

Once you're familiar with the top tips professional house flippers and investors use, we're moving on to turn our attention to a few characteristics of a house itself. When it comes to the way you should look at the process of buying and flipping homes in their entirety, this book runs similar to the buying process for the home. Before you begin to think about the advantages of a home it is essential to ensure that you've taken all the necessary steps prior to the purchase as well as be aware of your specific financial situation and wants. After you've read this chapter, you'll have a thorough understanding of the attributes that can be found in homes that you must not sell due to the fact that repairs can be costly and can take a lot of time to repair.

Property First Feature: Pools

At first, you might think the idea of having a pool on your investment property is something that is a great idea. If you decide to sell to a person who has kids you will be thrilled to provide their children with an area to play. From the perspective of an investor it is possible for a pool to cause a lot of trouble rather than a benefit of the house. The pool will not be able bring value to the property so you'll be required to cover the cost of this feature in advance when you purchase the property from the market. If you don't have any experience managing a pool you're likely be required to find someone with expertise in this field. In addition, if you're planning to lease out your house rather than sell it once you have fixed the problem, it's crucial to be aware that there are a lot of costs for insurance that come along with keeping a pool your backyard. If you're renting out your home to tenants, it means you'll be paying more for homeowner's insurance than needed. In certain states, it's mandatory to put up an enclosure around any space which has an area with a swimming pool. If your property doesn't yet have fence, it means you'll pay an additional amount of between 4,000 and 6,000 to put one up.

Property Feature 2: Asbestos

Asbestos should be considered due to the simple reality that homes that will be more affordable will likely to be older ones. Although asbestos isn't employed in the construction of homes today but it was an extensively utilized construction material that first began to be utilized in the mid-40s. Asbestos is an excellent material to build houses since it is very resistant to fire as well as an excellent sound and heat insulation; however, asbestos can be extremely cancerous when it is ingested into lung of a human. It's crucial to realize the fact that when asbestos exists present in an unconsolidated mass it's not likely to cause harm. The asbestos is when it begins to degrade into a powder that can easily penetrate the lungs, that it can become extremely harmful to human health.

The removal of asbestos from your home usually requires the use of a HAZMAT suit due to the simple reason that don't want to breathe in or be exposed to asbestos. In addition to having to have the right tools and equipment to get rid of the asbestos-containing particles, but you must ensure that you do it correctly. If, for instance, you decide to take asbestos out of a house by yourself You'll need be sure that the asbestos doesn't spread further throughout the affected area while you get rid of it. If you're not cautious, you could end up spreading asbestos to other areas of your home that could cause nothing but more issues. If you engage a contractor to eliminate asbestos from a structure for you, the cost could be more than 3000 dollars. This does not include the costs involved in conducting the tests in a lab, or a follow-up test following the time that the area is contaminated has been cleaned. Because of this, as a prospective property investor, it is recommended to avoid asbestos-related renovations as much as you can.

Property Features 3 Water Damage or Cracks

The last things we'll discuss are water damage and cracks. If you're considering buying the property, make sure to look at the structural components of the house. What you should perform when moving around an apartment is look at the doors and windows and the facade of the exterior of the house. When you examine the windows and doors and windows, look for cracks blocking either structure from shutting correctly. This is an obvious sign that there's an issue with the structural structure of the house. Also, if you go outside on the exterior of your home and see that there are cracks in the foundation that aren't moving with the mortar used to support the foundation of the house which means the home is breaking apart. Restructuring the structure of a house is costly because it involves working from scratch, and to rework parts of the structure which are supporting the house in different ways. Beware of properties that require these types of repairs.

Another thing you must be aware of when you visit a house which is for sale are indicators that water damages have occurred. The most obvious sign that there's been water damage to the property in the past can be observed within the basement (if there's basement). The basement's walls that have had water damages, are likely to be covered with staining and be stained in some way. The discoloration that occurs on the walls can be a sign that water tends to enter the home. When it is in the home there's no place where it can go. This can lead to flooding. This is an issue that is structural and you don't want to deal as an investor.

Chapter 4: Finding Great Deals

This pillar is just as crucial as financing and is tied in first to "financing". It is the basis that is "buying". It is crucial to be skilled in knowing how to buy homes when it comes to flipping them. You must be able to locate amazing deals, make excellent bargains, and buy houses that provide you with the greatest chance to earn back your investment and also make making a profit. In order to get funding, you'll have to ensure that you have a viable project in mind so that you can show the financier that you'll be able repay them.

There's plenty to learn about the process of buying houses, and it is crucial to be attentive and make an effort to becoming proficient and knowledgeable about this field. The more you understand how to do this, the better off you will be at purchasing homes that will offer the greatest opportunity to make a profit. This chapter will examine everything you should be aware of and will help you to feel more confident making deals and finding deals.

When you're looking to purchase an investment property to flip, there are four main questions you must answer first. Understanding the answer to those questions can assist you in deciding what you're looking to accomplish so that you can be sure that you're making the best choices and providing yourself with the best chance to earn a profit.

Answer #1: Which Type of House(s) will you buy?

The first thing to think about is which kind of homes you will purchase. This will allow you to develop your own niche within the house flipping industry. While it might not appear as though, picking the right niche and keeping a common "style" of the house that you are focusing on will provide you a huge advantage when you're getting into the market of house flipping. It will allow you to find trustworthy contractors and establish connections with them to ensure you have reliable people working on your home as well as provide you with the chance to gain knowledge about that particular type of house so that you can be sure that your projects are completed correctly and will meet the needs and requirements of the buyers who purchase these types of houses.

When you answer the question, you're likely to also want to look at where you stand within your business and what you are planning to accomplish. It's not a great idea to move into multi-family homes as a newbie however, if that is the goal for you in the future it is best to start smaller. Start small and allow you to master all the information you require to know to ensure that when you do venture into a bigger project, you'll be ready and equipped with the necessary knowledge to succeed in your flip.

The best kinds of homes to concentrate on are those which are between 1200 and

2,000 square feet in size and which have between 3 and 4 bedrooms. Although this isn't a set of rules that you must adhere to however, it gives you the chance to acquire the knowledge and experience prior to jumping into bigger and more expensive projects. Before you start exploring houses within this price range you'll need to think about what's typical in the neighborhood you're working in. In the end, there's no advantage to gaining experience in an area that isn't the "standard" house style of the neighborhood you want to live in. Let's take an example: the typical home in your neighborhood is around 1,000 square feet and includes two bedrooms. There's no reason to start working on a 500-square-foot bachelor pad. Neither would there is a reason for making an effort to remodel an 3,000 square foot mini-mansion. If you go outside of the area the market where your most significant market will be would be ineffective and could consume your energy, time and money. Consider what is required and desired in your area's housing market and then move on to the next. It is possible to switch the way you do it once you have more experience, but in meantime, concentrate on the things that are likely make you money.

Apart from considering the home's dimensions, you're likely need to consider conditions of your home and the condition of the house. You shouldn't invest into a property that is the most awful or worse state. The project could cost a lot of money and rapidly and dramatically reduce the profits. The most profitable projects to look for are those with a history of being "distressed" or require some repairs. It is not advisable to invest into something that requires major changes, however, particularly in the case of your very first residence. Also, you should avoid any property that requires significant structural changes or major renovations. For the first time, be sure to focus on houses that require cosmetic or minor repairs. In this way, you'll provide yourself with plenty of opportunities to learn about creating schedules and budgets as well as hiring contractors and setting yourself up to be successful. As you get more acquainted with how to flip houses, you may look into more costly options that, if executed correctly, could yield more money. But at first, these tend to eat into , or even totally squander your profit margins because of the lack of knowledge in the home flipping industry.

If you're following the same principle that you shouldn't buy something that will require a significant amount of money or expensive repairs. You are likely to also want to avoid older properties. Older homes typically require many more repairs than those of younger homes and, in the majority of cases, these repairs are costly. If you're not trained it's easy to overlook these possible repairs and you might not plan for these repairs. In the end, you may end up being under-funded or even short-changing your project. Instead of searching for homes that are very old, try to find ones that are only two or three years older. You shouldn't go too brand new as you're likely be spending more money to purchase it, and won't have the same chance of making profits on it.

It is crucial to realize that these rules aren't the final word on what you're getting into. They're great to listen to and follow but you're able to making your own judgement when you get to it. There is a chance that you will find projects that diverge from these guidelines , but can still be something you are able to manage or complete and generate a decent profit margin from. It is recommended to use your own judgment. The point for these rules is to to get you thinking about what you're doing and to ensure that you take into account all aspects, not only the superficial or fundamental ones. The more you can explore all aspects of the rehabs you'll be undertaking, the more easy it will be to buy into projects that are certain bring you some money.

Question 2: In What Region Will You Be Searching for these Houses?

After you've decided on the kinds of homes you would like to look at You must consider the exact location you plan on purchasing your homes. When you're deciding on the location you'd like to focus your attention you can pick from a small area to as extensive as multiple cities.

If you're starting out in the field, it is best to choose an area that is smaller like one city or an entire neighborhood. The final choice based on what you have learned about the house flipping business is, and what strategies you plan to employ to buy these homes. As your business expands and expands, the more you'll be able increase the size of the chosen location and acquire more houses in various cities or neighborhoods. But, when you're just starting out, it's much simpler to concentrate on one location at to begin and get acquainted with the region.

The reason you should choose to concentrate on this specific zone is because it's likely to provide you with an opportunity to network further. It will allow you to locate reliable contractors in this region and you'll be able to get acquainted with the desires and requirements of those who move to the region, and you will be able to gain an in-depth knowledge of the neighborhood as a whole. You'll know the most popular streets and what the typical valuation of homes is in the area and what you'll have to do to boost an increase in the worth of your house in accordance with the area and the demands of those who live or relocate to it. There's plenty to know about particular areas which is why the greater you know about them, the more success you'll have rehabilitating these homes and making profits from the properties. If you don't spend some time to learn these facts and you don't, you could be spending a lot of money for things that aren't needed in the area that you reside in. In the end, you may lose money.

An ideal goal in the beginning of this stream of income is to choose an area close to where you reside. This will give you the best chance to gain a lot of knowledge about your investment and projects, and also will make it simpler for you to collaborate with other individuals in order to finish your project. If you are in a location that's not ideal for flipping houses and you're looking for a better location, you'll need to choose an area which is close to your home as you can. This will make administration and many other aspects of your project simpler. It isn't easy to put long commute times on top of the other tasks that you have to take on when you begin your journey into house flipping.

Third Question: What Would You Provide for these Houses?

If you're preparing to negotiate a deal and are looking to make an offer, you must determine whether the deal is worthy one. While you're conducting the deal analysis, it is important to carefully determine how much you can afford to spend on an investment property, as well as all of the costs related to flipping the project. It is important to ensure you'll still be able to make an income over all the fees and expenses you incur for the deal. If there's no profits or a small amount this isn't the best deal to invest in.

If you don't spend the time to study what you need to know about how to analyze and evaluate the houses you're considering buying, you'll end up in a scenario in which you will not be in a position to earn any profits. It is important to understand how to distinguish a good deal from a poor one because the difference between the two is the possibility of making an income or end up in a deep gap of debt. It is not possible to be able to manage your business successfully if you don't make the effort to understand this vital aspect of the deal-making and home buying process.

The most important thing to consider when analyzing an offer is to find out What the value of the house after repairs (ARV) can be. It is the price you will advertise and sell the house when you're finished with the rehab process and the house is in its retail value. When you have this figure in mind, you'll be able to determine all the costs that take place in the process of acquiring and renovating the property. What are left with is the profit margin. If your profit margin isn't the way you want the future, then you might be able to modify or alter the other expenses to achieve the ideal profit ratio. If that isn't an option you're sure that the property isn't an ideal deal to invest in.

Question #4: What Strategies Are You Using to Locate and purchase these houses?

After you've determined what you'd like to buy and have figured out the price range and house you can manage, the next step is to take the plunge and purchase the house. To accomplish this, you're likely to have to research the exact property you wish to purchase into. There are a variety of ways to locate homes that are to purchase, but the most effective method is to search the Multiple Listing Service (MLS). You can learn about buying homes auctions and which houses are for sale within your budget and under the conditions you want and requirements. There are many alternatives to seek out bargains and you'll be able to discover more about these methods when you become more involved in the buying and reselling industry. Most often, you'll learn about sales via your network, which could be a good fit for you that is an excellent method to find great ideas for new ventures.

If you're looking to buy or sell a house it is important to understand that the process of buying isn't as straightforward as simply submitting the bid. It is essential to think about the way you plan to finance the house. This is the reason we have looked at various ways to finance. We hope that, after you have learned about these, you'll be able to put certain options in mind when you go to searching for homes. When you have decided on the method you will choose to buy the property and have secured your financing you can buy your home and start your new venture!

It is among of the most vital components of the home flipping process. It is essential to know about the buying process as much as you can, because this is the component of the process that's likely to either help you earn huge profits or leave your finances in the red. If you're buying a house and other properties, you must become proficient in determining which will yield a profit and which ones will drain your money and leave into nothing. It is crucial to to ask all the pertinent questions to make sure that the undertaking you're committing yourself to is worth the investment. It is recommended at the beginning to stick to the safe or conservative aspect of things, since it will help you avoid making costly mistakes which could cost your company before it has even begun.

In this chapter, you've been presented with four issues you should think about. The four questions:

What kind of home you would like to purchase?

Where would you like to purchase it?

What would you like to pay for it?

What are you planning to locate it in order to create your proposition?

It is essential to be able to answer these questions prior to embark on any venture in the sense that leaving one of them unanswered could lead to a costly mistake. The answers you get will provide you with an accurate and precise understanding of what you're getting into and what you have to do to earn an appropriate return. It's worth it to take the time to be prepared to answer these questions prior to deciding to decide to sign up for a deal and commit a significant amount of money in order to invest. If you dothis, you'll be more likely to run success and make you a significant gain as a result.

Flipping houses isn't difficult and it isn't even that difficult. However, it requires you to have a keen eye to understand the risks involved to ensure that you're getting an excellent profit which will help you make your flipping project profitable.

Chapter 5: Five Items That Will Make Your Flip Flop

Although flipping houses can be extremely lucrative, it is also a many risk factors too. Knowing these five common mistakes can help not turn your flip into a failure. A lot of successful investors made these errors. The price was so high that they nearly put them out of business following the first time they flipped. Therefore, follow the tips of the experienced flippers and be sure you're not making these mistakes that are common to flippers.

1. Over Enhance the House for the neighborhood

The majority of flippers started their businesses due to the desire to earn moneyand love to transform a beaten-up and dingy house into a gorgeous home. While it is important to enjoy your work, you shouldn't need to make the house too much better for the community. Consider the location and the buyer in mind as you make improvements. Do you think you could choose to install more costly and higher quality flooring to cause the house to appear more attractive and more appealing? Yes, but will that price increase your budget and cost you to take the home off the market? It might!

The best method to avoid the temptation to over-improve the home is to determine an amount that you will pay for each repair , and then refuse to spend more than that. If you've budgeted for flooring at $4,000, keep within that amount. It's astonishing how a small amount here and there can cost you your budget. Add all the "littles" together and they'll become a massive loss.

The goal isn't necessarily to be the most expensive home in the neighborhood. It's not a matter of Hollywood flipping houses; it's a fact. Your goal is to make the most profit you can. This means adhering to your initial strategy. When you shop, make sure you do it with a sensible approach. There's no reason to live in your home. It must look nice, fresh and clean and stand out to your buyers. Do not put million-dollar amenities in a home that costs $100,000.

2.Want to make all your Profits on One Flip?

The most important thing to ensure consistent turning a profit is flipping a variety of homes at a reasonable price and turn an adequate profit from each of them. A lot of newbies in the field are trying to make all their money on one turn, which is why they purchase a house that is expensive and invest a significant amount of cash into repairs, but then take a bite out of their profits due to the fact that they're required to keep the house longer than they anticipated. Flipping and buying expensive houses isn't necessarily a guarantee that you'll earn more cash. What it means is that you'll have to put more risk to "perhaps" gain more profit, possibly as the key word.

Profits can be taken in smaller chunks. Flip a few smaller houses and earn a profit of from $20,000 to $25,000 for each. This will be less stressful to manage your finances and your overall health. You'll feel less stressed with less money to lose. Additionally, your buyers' pool is bigger for moderate-priced houses and you'll be able to sell them more quickly. Repairs are typically much less expensive also. Practice flipping smaller houses before playing with the big boys flippers.

If you think about it, which is more profitable to flip one house to make a profit of $60,000 instead of flipping five small houses and earn $125,000 in profit? You can learn more about flipping houses through doing more, and flipping five homes will give you more benefits and experience than a larger or more expensive one.

3. Do not have the time to manage the Flip in a proper manner

Inexperienced managers attempt to flip houses even as they are working in full-time jobs. It is possible to flip houses and be a full-time worker when you're willing to grow your business more slowly and are patient in the process. There isn't as much income, but it's a way to ensure your financial independence and sanity. If you have to take on a second job full-time while you build your house flipping company Do not attempt to complete everything yourself. The stress and time could be the reason for your failure. Find a group of experts to complete the work and handle the task while you are working your regular job.

Some flippers are trying to get their hands dirty and improve their flips during the weekend. In the end, what was an effort of love, is turned into a series of "honey to" weekends. Then you realize that you do not want to leave for the location and work isn't completed. Successful and timely flipping requires an individual to keep an check on the development. Since the time you spend flipping is money, each second you're exhausted can affect your profits.

In addition to the time lost as well, but it's hard to supervise your construction team and supervise the quality of work if you're not present. If you're planning to work your regular job while flipping then you should think about hiring a partner to handle the flips full-time. A 50/50 partnership doesn't mean that your earnings are cut in half. If a reliable and responsible partner lets you turn houses faster for more profit and to flip more houses in a shorter amount of time it could mean you earn a significant portion of money over the long term.

4.Begin Flipping with a Little Knowledge and even less Skill

It's hoped that this isn't your case because after studying this book, you have already shown an interest in learning prior to entering into the business selling houses. Thank you! You're an inch ahead of other once-in-a-lifetime flippers. But don't let this book become your sole source of knowledge. Continue reading and attend events and meetings with investors. Find mentors open to sharing their experience and wisdom.

In every business, there is competition But don't view the competition as having an adverse effect on your ability to expand and grow your business. It sharpens you and keeps you current with market trends. Find out what's popular to repair and ways to save money on furniture. Learn what prospective buyers are asking for, and then add the items you want to flip to your own flips. Research what kind of houses are the easiest to sell and purchase these. Don't sit around waiting in the hope that the market will shift take action and stay ahead of the game.

Make every opportunity to develop new techniques that can help your to make savings on your next opportunity. Keep an eye on your skilled laborers and keep an eye on their secrets to reducing costs.

Look at homes and discover what draws buyers, while another property with the same value is in the marketplace. Note that some repairs won't be able boost the value of the property however they can give your property the "WOW" factor that draws the attention of realtors(r) and buyers. In the end, these techniques can increase your profits since they aid in selling the house faster.

5.Step off of the Math

Refusing to adhere to your original strategy is the biggest error that flippers make. It's not because they do not know the best price they can afford while still making profits, but it's making repairs that are more costly that cause new flippers to get into danger. They have budgeted a certain amount but then start to compromise their budget for various items. In no time the numbers are upside down which means you're left with a the house that you aren't able to sell at the price you'd like.

There is no way to compromise on the math. Make sure you make no changes to the amount you believe you will get for your house following the repairs. This is a risky game to are playing when you start to justify the need for more expensive repairs to a home in the hope of getting more money when you decide to sell it.

Many of these errors happen because you've allowed yourself to be too emotionally involved with your home. It's true that we're trained to be awed by homes. Home is where our heart is and the place where our most precious childhood memories are stored. We tend to think of homes as a place where we feel peace as well as security and security. It's not difficult to understand the reason why there is a desire to make your property the most desirable within the neighborhood. But the idea of thinking of your property the same way you would your personal home is going to hinder you from making appropriate improvements and make the highest income.

We cannot stress this enoughIt's a business! Take your mind in and let your heart go. There are many entrepreneurs who say they invest their soul and heart into their ventures to make it grow. Now, we're telling to apply your business brain and logic into your business , and put your emotions aside. Don't buy a house just because you're over in love with the property. Do not select products based on exactly what you'd like to have in your house. Choose your products based on what can yield the most profit in the least amount of time.

The most costly mistake is letting fear stop you from making a move. A few people are intrigued by the idea of flipping homes, and they read about it, and fantasize about doing it , but they never make the leap. What a shame that you allow fear to hinder your being successful. Experience and knowledge are the most effective ways to conquer your fears. It's natural to be scared of the risk. Flipping houses does entail taking chances. If it were that simple then you'd spend all your time fighting against the other house flippers. Everyone would be making money flipping houses.

As we face the challenges of life and tackling issues, it's the time to recognize that flipping houses isn't as easy as it appears seen on TV. It's not typical to turn the house around in two months. You won't always sign a contract on the first day you put the property open. Also, as sad as it is that you will not always earn an enormous profit. For some, you'll are keeping your fingers crossed with the hope of making even. You aren't going to be in your Sunday clothes to tidy up after yourself. You'll have to clean a majority of the filth of others and you'll encounter several mysterious pests hidden under the surface of everything! One of the worries that you'll have to fight is fear of unwelcome residents. Ask any investor and they will be happy to share their stories of horror of flips. You might find people living in your back bedroom, insects dead animals, leftovers from teenage parties and all kinds of leftovers from previous events. But don't fret; you'll be ready for any eventuality in advance. You'll be able to smell the problems before they occur.

Okay, if you've gone through this far and are still wanting to flip houses, then you're prepared for your next move. When you earn between $25,000 and $50,000 from a renovation that's worth it, everything's worth it.

Chapter 6: How Is The Best Place To Look For Houses That Are Suitable To Flip

One of the first hurdles when flipping houses is how to find suitable homes. The first step is to select from foreclosure houses or browse through the MLS online or through the information provided with local agents. But, there are many other less well-known sources you could consider. This list will assist you in finding the right houses to sell.

Probate house sales

Probate sales are excellent source of homes for flipping because the properties are offered for sale at an affordable price. In some cases, those who are interested are looking to have their property that was inherited turned into cash as quickly as they can This is where you are able to help.

Individual sellers can post online listings

There are people on the internet who are in in need of money and selling their properties directly to anyone who might be interested. This deal will cut out the costs for real estate agents this is an advantage for you. The advertisement can be published on the blog of the person website, social media sites or other websites of which he is a part of.

Property Wholesalers

Wholesalers of houses are excellent sources for houses to sell. They also can offer lower rates for houses as a whole. All you have to do is find out which wholesalers in your area are.

Multiple Listing Service (MLS)

As I said before I suggested that you search the house listings on MLS online, which comprises all the houses available for sale. There are a variety of MLS websites. Some of my favorite are ZipRealty.com along with TheMLS.com. It is possible to conduct an advance search to determine the range of prices you are able to manage and the amount of rooms or other information you require. Based on the results, you will be able to choose the most suitable property to sell. When you are in the initial phases of the process, in which you write the business strategy, it's beneficial to conduct a little small amount of research using MLS houses to understand the prices and estimates for the property within a specific region.

Auctions of properties on hold because of tax issues

These are properties which have been placed in limbo due to tax concerns. The sheriff in your area will typically have information about these auctions. They are usually put on sale during an auction that is scheduled for a particular date, and once you've won the tax payer still has a specific amount of time to pay their tax due. If you do, then you won't receive the property. If they don't do, they are kicked out and the property becomes yours. The procedure varies across cities, so make sure to inquire with your county official since it might be different there.

Other listings online

There are other websites that help you connect with an agent selling property. The cost can be higher but because the middleman that is the website usually charges fees. The most popular websites to use are: Zillow.com and Homes.com. A quick internet search will provide you with a list of websites that will connect you to sellers in your local area.

Local newspaper

The most reputable local paper will certainly have a homes for sale in your area. Select one from the list and make an ocular inspection to see if the house is suitable to flip.

Television

Television is an excellent source of homes for sale. Make sure you have a pencil and paper to list the phone names and postal addresses.

Radio

If you are unable to pay for the high costs of television and written advertisements Radio is an ideal option. Radio can be used to be a great way to reach the community in which you live and also allow you to do deals with house owners.

The most important thing to keep in mind when searching for property is to avoid rushing. Make sure you take the time to research and look over all houses in your area and assess using an experienced estimator.

Chapter 7: What Do Earn 6 Figures In Real Estate?

The investment in real estate can assist in increasing the flow of cash. If you can become a skilled investor, you will be earning six figures with your investments. But, in order to achieve this, you have to know the many elements of real estate investing, develop an effective strategy and complete the essential tasks to achieve your financial freedom. There are many steps you need to take to be successful as an investor and these are listed below.

Change Your Thinking Concerning Making Investments

The success of your business is as dependent on your actions as your mental attitude. A positive mindset is essential for becoming an investor who is successful. In this article you'll learn the reasons why a

9-5 job isn't what it appears to be, common misconceptions regarding money mindsets and how you can change your views about money, the behaviors you need to develop to be an expert investment property owner, ways to alter your perspective and the myths that surround making passive income.

Learn More About Real Estate Making a Profit

This section you'll be taught the fundamentals of flipping a house including what it means and the advantages it can bring as well as its drawbacks, the potential risks and ways to reduce those risks, ways to determine your goals and the outcomes you hope to accomplish through investing in real estate and ways to accomplish your objectives.

Learn the secrets to success In Real Estate. Real Estate Industry

Within this article, you'll discover some of the most important factors in the business which will determine the success of your investment The most common pitfalls that you should be aware of and the best way to find the most lucrative deals on property, and the things that you could do in order to make sure that you're treated with respect in your role as an investment.

Find the right property to invest in

If you don't have the right home to purchase, you will not become a successful investment. Within this article, you'll discover the different individuals you should engage: a property management or real estate agent, an inspector for homes, a handyman along with an attorney. Learn about creating an orderly timeline when looking for a property, ways you can find flippable properties, the various properties to pick from as well as the laws that apply to them, and other factors external to the property.

Learn all the aspects that are involved when looking at and purchasing an Investment Property.

Within this article, you'll discover the aspects you must consider when looking at the properties you might want to purchase, as well as the process of crunching figures regarding the property, methods to acquire the required investment capital, the various ratios you can determine, as well as the various strategies you can employ to seal the deal.

Steps to Make Money

In order to begin earning profits from the property, you must boost the value of your property. This means that you have to find cost-effective methods to increase the margin of profit while ensuring that you're getting your value from your property as well as the services provided by the contractors you hire. Here, you'll discover the various aspects to be addressed before purchasing properties, and the simple changes you'll need to carry out when flipping a property, regardless of whether you choose to go with an DIY method or employ an expert to assist negotiate with an expert contractor, and re-designing the exterior of the building with a low-cost approach.

Make sure you have an exit strategy in place or a backup plan in case Things Don't Go As Planned

An experienced investor will always have a backup plan for when things go wrong. You should be aware of the risks you're taking, and prepare an alternative plan that you are able to apply immediately when you suspect that the market is changing. If you're keen on flipping homes, you must learn how to sell your property. If you aren't able to find the perfect buyer it is important to understand how you can save your investment. You need to know how to conclude an agreement. In addition you should be prepared for the eventuality that every real estate investor fears What do you do if something goes wrong? If you don't plan for this, then you're placing yourself in danger of failing. It is also important to be aware of the most common errors to avoid when investing in real property.

You'll learn more about each step in the next chapters. Following these steps, you'll be able achieve financial security and independence while also becoming an effective investor.

Chapter 8: Creating An Action Plan

You've now got an estimated budget and a group and now it's time to purchase your home. Because you've engaged the accountant CPA as well as a realtor in the budgeting stage Your team will be able assist you in finding and purchasing your home. In this chapter, we'll discuss how to go through this stage. It's time to have fun!

Locating your home

Keep in mind that your first home is supposed to be a simple one. You don't want to overburden yourself or exceed your budget. Select a home that requires the least amount of repairs. After narrowing down to one or two, you'll need to consult an appraiser to verify that your asking prices are correct to ensure you don't pay too much for the flip. It is a good idea to find out what the house could be worth once it's completed. Now let's discuss how to choose the perfect property.

Market research is the time to decide the location you intend to purchase. Your realtor will help you determine the best location to fit your budget. Find out what houses are bought and sold for in each region. It is also important to determine which your market likely to be. In 2016, for instance, more Millennials bought homes and baby boomers are selling more. This indicates that it's an excellent idea to pick an area that you could focus on younger generations. Are property values increasing or decreasing? Is the region expanding? Gentrification is a wonderful opportunity for home flippers. It is possible to purchase a home when the prices for housing remain low and then then market it at a premium in the wake of the new market which is flooding the area. If the area is likely to be booming in the coming few years, you may prefer to keep your home as a rentalproperty, but sell it when the area is highly sought-after.

You can make use of free sites such as Zillow or Trulia to look over every property within the neighborhood, and learn about crime rates, schools and the value of property. You can also consult your local MLS (Multiple Listing Service) which is a comprehensive listing of homes that are available through brokers.

Simplify the processAfter you've found the location you are looking for, pick 3 or 4 houses. Conduct a thorough investigation on the properties to determine whether there are any lien (if the seller is owed money either in tax or another obligation, the property may belong to the creditor till the debt is settled). If you purchase a property that has a lien attached to it the property, you'll be held accountable for the amount owed. Check to see if you have paid your taxes and current, otherwise you will be liable for any tax back that may be due. It is advisable to get a survey plan and also to view the boundaries and information about geography of the property.

Take a tour of each house. Bring your realtor and contractor along. They are experts in their field and can spot hidden problems which could cost you money. Only a professional will determine if there's mold, asbestos or damages to your foundation, and this is something that you should not take on. The professional will also be able provide an estimate of how much repair you can perform yourself, which can save you thousands of dollars. Inspectors for homes are expensive, but they'll be able to provide you with the most thorough assessment of the home and highlight any significant issues and the things that need to be addressed to ensure compliance.

Create a scheduleSet a timetable on the job when the house is yours. Working with your contractor on putting the timeline together will ensure consistency and efficiency. It is not a good idea to drag the process out by doing things in a non-conformist order, or by not remembering particulars. Remember, time is money particularly in the business world.

It's time to pick your home! You have all the info you need and you've got your budget in place and you've spoken to the experts. As we've mentioned it is important to select the home that has the lowest cost as well as the most minimal amount of repairs. This is a choice that must be taken by your contractor. Before buying there are some frequent mistakes you should be sure to avoid:

Not budgeting properly. Making and adhering within your spending plan is crucial to the results the flip. Without a budget, will definitely overspend more than you ought to, and could lose cash on a flip if you're not careful.

Do not overuse the pros. Certain things should be left to experts. If you're not a licensed real estate agent (which is a good option if you're into the business of flipping) there's plenty of knowledge and expertise that you do not have. The realtor you hire knows the market and has the potential to sell and is able to sell your home much faster than you will. Your team should work with you. Be smarter and not more. Do not make mistakes yourself! It will be costing you more than hiring for a professional.

A property that is overpriced. Although it's more exciting to purchase an enormous home in a desirable area, this could be your first time flipping. Foreclosures and bargain houses are the ideal place to begin. The larger houses can be expensive to buy, and there's lots of property to fix and remodel. In addition, you must wait for a buyer who is wealthy, which could take a long time. Keep your budget in check as well as let the accountant assist you. Your realtor may make a better offer than you could.

Don't bother with the research. If you aren't sure of what you're buying , then it's difficult to know the risks you're getting into. If you purchase a property in a location where property values are falling, you could be losing money. If you purchase a home that is asbestos-based, you're likely to pay thousands in repair costs just for that. You could also end up with an enormous tax lien when you purchase the home. Conduct all the research you can and , again, ask your team to assist you.

The pool can be an appealing asset initially. You might think that it can make the asking price increase and bring buyers in competition for your home. Yes, a pool can bring value to your home, but this means that the price you pay will be higher. Consider the costs of renovating the pool and bringing it up to standards, and the insurance costs will consume your profits. If you are planning to lease the house out the rules and regulations are extremely complicated and costly. Pools are a potential danger and is recommended to stay clear of it.

Chapter 9: Tips To Consider Prior To Purchasing An Investment Property

If you've gained a bit knowledge about the kind of financial considerations you need to think about when you are preparing to purchase your first home to flip, we'll then turn our attention to the most important tips top house flippers utilize and employ when flipping houses. Once you're aware of these guidelines that are available, you'll equipped to apply these tips as you go through the process of researching and buying process of purchasing a house to flip. Let's look at the most important strategies immediately.

Investment Tips for Property 1: Stick to Your Budget

When you're more familiar in calculating your ARV, you'll be at ease with the calculation of how much you'll be spending on your home. When you have a reasonable number that you're willing and able to spend it is important to be sure to stay within that number. Many new investors fall in love with one particular property, only to attempt to make the purchase possible by shifting funds and delaying spending elsewhere in their lives. Try to avoid making this mistake. Once you've got your budget in place, adhere to it. That means even if you come across the perfect home that you fall in the love with, if the price is out of your budget, then you must get rid of it. While you're going through this process, you need to keep in mind that you're looking for a property that you can flip and not one which you have to completely enjoy because it isn't the right one ideal for you. Be calm and keep your emotions in check so you'll get one step closer to achieving an investment property that is successful.

Investment property Tip 2: Select the right Neighborhood

In the realm of real estate there are generally three kinds of neighborhoods available in the marketplace. The neighborhoods are described just by the letters "A", "B" and "C". Let's examine every type of neighborhood right to determine which neighborhood you're looking for a house in:

Neighborhood A Neighborhood A is one of the neighborhoods comprised of mostly single-family homes. Neighborhoods of this type are best described as ones are found in a posh neighborhood. A typical example of neighborhood is an area with a gated entrance or a community composed of individuals who make the six-figures and have two kids and also have a person who trims their lawn each week. There aren't many tenants in these communities.

Neighborhood B kind of neighborhood is known as a working-class community. If you walk through this type of community there is a good chance that you'll find working trucks and vans parked in driveways. Another indicator to tell you that it's a class B neighborhood is the presence of duplexes, multi-family homes and duplexes located throughout the area.

Neighborhood C kind of neighborhood is quite shabby and deteriorating. In a C type community it is more likely that there will be a possibility that the tenants of the house could find themselves in a situation where they're unable to pay their rent and you'll be in the unfortunate position of owning a property that is vacant.

Neighborhood Type B is the ideal kind of neighborhood when looking to flip the home. If are an expert contractor and you know that you are able to transform the house that is in need of repair to a property which can compete in an A-type neighborhood then great job However, for a lot of homeowners who are new to flipping houses, this the case. A B-type neighborhood can provide you with the chance to make as denser a decision as you can in your exit strategy and in this kind of community, the residents will likely to be the most accommodating of your presence within their neighborhood.

Investment Property Tip 3: Be aware of the size

This advice is fairly simple. If you're planning to flip your first home it is important to be sure to keep the magnitude of your venture in your mind. What's the reason you would want to take on massive homes when you've never done such a task before? Start small and, when you're enjoying your work, you can slowly progress to flipping houses that are huge and bring you more profits.

4. Investment Property Tips: be wary of the short sale

If a homeowner decides it's wise to stop making his mortgage for some reason or another then the lender is likely to take over the property. This is obviously a difficult thing for the bank to handle since they're basically taking over the debt the homeowner was previously owed. If there is remaining debt that needs to be transferred to the bank in relation to this property lender will attempt to sell it at a reduced price since there's less debt to be paid back than what would be the case with the typical mortgage. Although this might seem like an excellent opportunity to profit from an investment standpoint but the reality is the bank will not sell you a house at a discount when they can. In this case and it is not uncommon for it to take a longer period for the bank to transfer the property to you, so you'll be waiting to begin making progress on it and flipping it. A good short sale can be purchased quickly by a seasoned and experienced property investor. Although it's an ideal idea to begin understanding how short sales operate but when you're getting started, it's an ideal idea to steer clear of short sales.

Investment Property Tip 5: Keep in mind that the one Percent Rule

If you're planning to flip a house and lease it out, instead of selling it to a third party and earning a profit by doing this and making a profit, then you must consider the one-percent rule. This rule is useful to figure out if you're making the right investment prior to buying the property. To determine this the only thing you need to do is to take the cost of the property, and multiply this amount by .01. Let's say you purchase an investment property for rental that costs $225,000. That means that if you plan to let it out and earn a decent income from it, you'll have to rent your tenant at least $2250 per month for rent. If you're unable to charge this monthly rent, you're probably not buy the property that you are considering.

Chapter 10: What To Purchase

There are a variety of factors that influence the selection of the right regions where you can flip homes. It can be difficult to pick the most profitable area due to the market's trend changes every year.

In order to make money in the field of investing you have to devote a lot of time conducting extensive study. The most suitable place to hand your house over isn't always easy to determine and there are a variety of things to think about.

Furthermore, some markets that seemed to be temporarily great locations to flip houses later became crowded and were no longer attractive. This is why the most successful investor invests their time identifying promising areas where they can flip their house instead of rushing into the current trends.

Markets in which the unemployment rate is at or below a certain level must be taken into consideration and are also accompanied by substantial job growth. These conditions could be caused by the emergence of rapidly growing industries as well as notable companies within the region. Both of these are indicators of economic growth that boost home buying activity as well as the final increase in the value of assets.

It is also essential to consider whether there are good communities in areas where people are looking to settle. It is also important to make sure there is plenty of inventory available in the market.

If these requirements have been met, you are able to concentrate on financial aspects like the median price for purchase and the local average of cost of retrofit and labor. These numbers aid investors in determine post-repair valuation (ARV) and profits margin estimates.

It is crucial to exercise the importance of due diligence since positive economic indicators don't necessarily indicate favorable conditions for flippers of houses. If, however, you spot an area that is promising growth in the economy and lucrative profits, you are able to be confident when beginning an inquiry for property.

Determine the area you want to buy.

The best location to sell the house over isn't necessarily the one that offers the most potential profits, but rather in the areas where you can earn profits all over the world.

The three most popular markets to reverse housing in 2018 included South Dakota, Indiana, and Texas.

The most profitable market for turning homes typically offers a profit margin that is greater than the cost of admission.

One of the most effective methods to accomplish this is to examine patterns of the past to anticipate what direction the housing market might be in the near future. Based on Attom Data Solutions in the year 2000, US housing flippers earned an average of more than $65,000 per home.

Be aware that profit margins can differ significantly from one place to the next and the best market shifts every year. Below is a list of the cities considered the most attractive to reverse housing prices in recent years. Do you have a good idea of the best market for 2019?

EL PASO, TEXAS

El Paso, Texas is among the top spots on the list of top areas to flip houses in the year 2018. This is because of its incredible potential for market growth. As per U.S. News, Texas's location scores 7.2 /10 for the quality of life. This places as the 5th retirement destination within the United States.

According to Zillow According to Zillow, more that 70 Fortune 500 companies are based in the region, and is considered to be the fourth largest manufacturing hub within the United States. The median home value was $ 123,400. This is which is an improvement of 3.6 percent from prior year.

These numbers, combined with the low retrofit and renovation cost in this region gave investors with a substantial ROI potential.

OKLAHOMA CITY, OKLAHOMA

Oklahoma City is known as an economic hub in the region in a wide range of areas, such as medical services, information technology and the government. Oklahoma City regained the top position in real estate ranking due to affordable home renovations and remodeling costs as well as the high living conditions.

Oklahoma City is the best city in which to start a new business. It is also a major indicator of population, economic and growth in housing.

PEORIA, ARIZONA

It is a fact that this Arizona city is among the most affordable places to renovate and upgrade assets in the nation. The median price of homes has been steadily increasing over the last six years.

SIOUX FALLS and SOUTH DAKOTA

The city is dubbed "America's Best Little City", Sioux Falls is a highlight of low-cost home renovations and homes with relatively low cost ($ 183,000). It is also praised by major financial institutions and an established regional medical industry.

The location was promising, with an excellent living quality and an 8.8 percent increase in the home's value within a year.

What should you buy

In flipping houses, the objective should be to buy the house at an extremely low cost and fix it up to sell it at the profit. When you purchase houses that are affordable in value will need you to repair the house prior to selling it. These are the kind of homes that you ought to look for and purchase.

Disseminated Property

The most important thing to do when flipping a home is to locate the property suffering from a lot of stress. The price of a damaged property is usually according to market values, and often require foreclosure or some sort of work.

Owners of homes may be unable to locate because they would prefer to be labelled as a victim. However, research will aid you in finding the treasure you've been searching for.

Here are some ways to identify distressed traits:

Abandoned HOUSE, UNOCCUPIED HOUSE, OR

It might be difficult to locate however, every city has an empty house. There are a variety of reasons the house is empty and each one could be an opportunity.

Owners who live out of town relocated to a different town and then left the property vacant instead of attempting to rent the property or even sell it. This may not be a top priority for them.

Real estate owned by banks: real Estate was seized and a lot of the property is empty. Banks are extremely interested in the collection of real estate balances and you'll usually find quite a bit.

Government property: Much like the property of banks These are the results of foreclosure. They can be seen on websites of the government.

Test for Will: If in the instance of a homeowner deceased and the heirs are not from the area or has no spouse, the home may be unoccupied and available to auction. Property for probation can be found at the county registry.

DELINQUENT OWNERS

Arrears may be due to mortgage or tax payment.

Arrears on mortgages: When you get a foreclosure notice the majority of homeowners leave their houses because they are unable to pay the arrears.

Tax Property confiscated due to tax unpaid as well as the property owner expelled the property will remain vacant up to the time the city decides whether to auction it. The properties are available on the Tax Assessor's Office.

LISTINGS

There are many homes that is priced under market value using MLS search, however it's extremely rare in certain areas. Another option is looking at websites that list the properties that are sold by the owner.

Take a look at local newspapers and Craigslist to locate a house similar to this. The sellers are very driven to sell their possessions immediately.

SENIOR CITIZENS

The elderly homeowners can no longer maintain their home, so they are usually seeking to move to smaller homes that are more manageable. They are generally willing to participate in direct marketing campaigns and there are seniors with direct mailers.

There are numerous ways to discover distressed assets. connect with people as well as let people know about what you're doing. Be on the lookout for things because you might find something in the streets of the city before you know it.

PRE FORECLOSURES, AND A Notice of Deficit

If a landlord fails to make your mortgage payments first, the lender will issue a Notice of Default to inform you of the due amount and giving you a specific timeframe during which you may pay.

If the owner fails to pay by the deadline the property will be sold to a distressed owner. is scheduled to take place for the property. Notice of default Notice of Default marks the beginning of the pre-foreclosure time.

The property owner can stop the sale at any point prior to the date of sale, by paying the full amount due on the loan. Consequently, some owners choose to sell their houses when they are in financial trouble by themselves.

This helps them stay out of foreclosure, which can be a significant impact on your credit in the long run. However, since owners of the home is required to only pay for the balance for the loan, and not the entire amount, they are able to sell the property at a price less than the value to ensure the sale and have enough cash to pay the obligation.

This results in great discounts for investors and buyers as well as excellent opportunities for homeowners who are with financial problems who want to stay out of foreclosure.

SALE AND AUCTIONS OF PROPERTIES in a variety of difficulties

If the homeowner is unable to sell the property prior to the date set to be auctioned off as foreclosure and the property is sold at an auction, either by the loan company or someone else you are able to trust.

The foreclosure auctions or house issues are the most popular method by which buyers can acquire homes that are foreclosed to sell. Auctions are held frequently across the country and are one of the fastest ways to purchase property of any kind.

All you need to be able to do is attend the auction day and be prepared to bid . If you win the house will be yours. It is of course an excellent opportunity to purchase houses at low cost in foreclosure auctions.

You should ensure that the financing upfront in order to be able to make the payment for the winning bid. Additionally, you should conduct thorough research about the properties you wish to purchase in order to make sure they are safe and an investment worth it.

However, whether you're an expert in buying homes for sale, land for sale , or property with certified problems or beginner, you will find that the auction procedure differs from the one of a normal real estate auction.

There is no need to speak with an agent, and you'll be issued a Sales Invoice as shortly as the auction closes. It's a great option to purchase a home or homes at auction as much as 60% less than what they are worth, the discounts are higher than what you will find and everywhere else.

REO HOUSING and BANK OWNED HOUSES

In the event that a foreclosure auction can not attract a buyer and the bid that is accepted falls less than a specified "minimum amount" amount that is set by the auctioneer the home will be handed over to the lending institution at close in the course of auction.

The lender, typically an institution like a bank or a government agency, can then have complete control of the property and then put it for sale on its own.

They are also known as REO (real estate owned) or bank property (real estate owned by). Nearly all banks offer properties that are reclaimed, however the issue is that they do not have the time or resources to market or advertise these properties.

Instead, local agents display the homes available to be sold. Purchase properties that are in need of sale, home sales and REO provide the same amazing discounts that any other investment in real estate that faces problems.

The banks typically offer these properties for less than their actual value to dispose of the properties, and those or investors looking to purchase a home will receive excellent deals.

THE PROCESS OF FORCLOSURE

Before you begin buying foreclosure properties, it is important to understand what foreclosure is. It is the method through which a lender tries to recover the amount owed from a mortgage with a delinquent balance.

If the property owner fails to not pay his loan installments and the lender is unable to meet the loan, it can take possession of its property to secure the loan. The next step is when you may decide to purchase foreclosure homes or foreclosed houses.

It's a very simple issue. When a mortgage is approved the house serves as collateral. Therefore, if the mortgage payment is not made in a timely manner, the property is auctioned off or sold by the lender.

Understanding the PROCESS OF FORECLOSURE

1. HOW FORECLOSURE STARTE?

Foreclosure Initiation generally occurs when a homeowner borrower fails to pay the required mortgage payment. If this occurs, based on the installments that are due the lender may decide to demand debt repayment within a specific period of time. And in the event that this timeframe is not fulfilled the foreclosure process begins.

In order to begin with the process of foreclosure, lenders has to provide public requirements for payment in writing to the debtor. This formal requirement, referred to as a default notice or a litigation notice is crucial to establish that the borrower is conscious of any debt that is owed towards the loaner.

If you're looking to buy the type of house it is possible to get advantages over the open market however, before you purchase a house with foreclosure, it is important to know how the process of selling these kinds of homes work. It is essential to maintain. You will require the data you'll need to look for such properties and understand exactly what the value of these properties is currently.

STEP 2: PROCESS OF FORECLOSURE

If homeowners know they have unpaid debt prior to foreclosure and are unable to make the amount due, they may opt to sell the home before foreclosure can take place.

In this particular instance, we're discussing the possibility that the seller is able to sign a sale contract with the buyer prior to the time of the sale.

So, he doesn't risk being a victim of foreclosure on his credit record, and the pre-seizure process is an advantage for the borrower or the default homeowner. This is crucial for the future as it can be very difficult to obtain new funds from the future with foreclosure and previous foreclosure.

If you are looking to purchase in advance foreclosures, you could enjoy a significant discount since the cost of selling is usually 20 to 60% less than the current market value. This is an advantage for those who wish to buy a home or invest in a property to the future. Another benefit is knowing beforehand everything that is related to the title of your property and avoid any unexpected surprise.

Step 3: FORECLOSURE AUCTIONS

If the pre-execution time period of the auction mortgage mortgage runs out and the loan is not paid The loan will be continued to take care of the mortgage.

From now from now it will then be sold through a public auction where prospective buyers can make bids.

Auctions for residential properties usually pay off the debt within real estate. In that instance the process is concluded by making a payment to the lender and the property becomes the property of the winning bidder.

To comprehend the foreclosure property auction procedure, the first step is distinguish between legal and judicial auctions. Each state sets its own rules regarding this.

It is vital to know the rules that apply to the state you have to bid for.

When you're bidding on auctions, the first thing to do is determine which homes are taking part in the auction within the state you'd like to purchase the property. An excellent option is to search for regularly updated and regularly published lists.

Auction bidding is a bit complicated and therefore you must gather enough details. In most cases the event that you are bidding on a home it will ask you to pay for a part or even the whole house so ensure that you have enough funds or money.

A crucial aspect to think about when bidding on any auction, is the need to thoroughly examine the value of the property to ensure that you don't spend more than the real worth of the house. If you don't wish to be paying more than you expected to then mark your maximum bid , and don't go higher.

There are not many options for inspecting properties or finding property titles. This is why you must get advice from an expert on the subject.

STEP 4: BANK OR GOVERNMENT ASSET RECOVERY (REO)

It is worth noting that banks and government agencies might hold the title of loans that are not paid and, consequently, all are able to perform foreclosure.

However, it's worth noting that the auction's bid could be substantially lower than the amount of your debt, or you might not be able to bid. In such cases, the bank or the government might decide to withdraw from the auction and take the property to add it to the portfolio of properties. This is part of the process known as REO.

If a lender has to take back its property because of default, the best option is to dispose of it in order to pay back an unpaid obligation. In this scenario an agent for real estate is able to sell government or bank assets and seeks buyers willing to pay to protect loss to the lender.

The advantage of purchasing this kind of property from a bank or the government is that the home is in excellent condition generally because they invest in necessary improvements and repairs. The kind of improvements can raise the price of the house but the gains you can earn are a bit lower.

Benefits of Buying a Foreclosure HOME

If you choose to invest in this type of property be aware that there are many advantages.

One is the possibility of acquiring excellent real estate with a more affordable cost on the market for real estate than the retail price.

You may also discuss with the buyer prior to purchase about the best possible terms for both of you to be successful.

If your goal is to invest money to make profit from selling property in the near term buying a home that is foreclosed is definitely the best choice. Think about the cheap price that foreclosure homes can fetch purchases , and consider the earnings you could earn through future auctions.

Chapter 11: Significant And Not So Important Fixes That Need To Be Made

It is recommended to have the most significant repair or renovation tasks completed in a priority order. This will prevent anxiety if you notice your budget going over limit since you'd have completed all major projects and then need to focus on minor tasks.

What are the most significant work or important repairs that need to be given attention to? The majority of experts agree that kitchens and bathroom are two areas that need to be dealt with first. Although appearance matters structural issues, clearing builders' inspections are some of the most important problems that need to be solved. Apart from these important issues, some of the main fixes are identified below to help you:

* Rewiring the house to avoid electrocution

Repairing damaged fixtures such as bathtubs, sinks and showers

* Patching ceilings, walls, door holes

* Repainting damaged or peeling paintwork

* Removing damaged tiles, pavers, steps

* Removing loose or broken brackets, hinges and fittings

Minor repairs include replacing modern fittings with existing but older fittings, painting better colors on decent paintwork, adding additional storage in cupboards, or cabinets, etc. These aren't required, particularly when you're limited in time and resources.

The reading of books that are relevant to the subject, which can be found in a variety can help you with this. One of the most cost-effective ways to boost the value of your house is by cleaning, painting, or using ornamental plants and replacing fixtures and fittings that are damaged or broken.

Cleaning and minor repairs completed by cheap laborers like college students or you If you can, it will allow you in saving money. Also, things like re-carpetingor retouching older fixtures, painting your front door, installing new handles, or repaving the patio, etc. can be done at a low cost.

Staging the House

Staging helps sell houses more quickly and this becomes an important factor when flipping a house. It's obvious that buyers would rather see a home lively and alive instead of examining empty, cold rooms when searching to find a new home.

In contrast to the widespread belief that staging is a costly alternative, below are some suggestions to help the homeowner to know how to stage the house efficiently and at low a price as is possible.

Select and choose the rooms There is no need for you to decorate every single room of the home. In fact it will be extremely expensive to do this. It is important to provide prospective buyers some idea about how they could utilize the space in the most appealing and efficient way. The following rooms could be furnished with the appropriate type of furniture:

* Master Bedroom

* Dining Room

* Living Room/Family Room

* Home Office

* Any room with an uneasy arrangement

The criteria for the size of the rooms could be rearranged and you may include or exclude any of the above based on the situation. If you have a patio, or an outdoor space could be included in the rooms that are to be staged. You can place a set of chairs and a table in the lawn that could allow the buyer to get some peaceful and refreshing ideas.

Set the budget and stick to it: It's important to ensure that you don't buy too much furniture for staging your home. Create a budget and factor all possible costs into it prior to buying the furniture. Here are some points to think of when planning the budget:

* The number of times that it will be employed

* Payment to the movers, and storage

* Qualitative aspect of furniture

If you intend to start a house flipping business and you're pretty certain of success in it, then it is sensible to purchase the required furniture that can be used repeatedly for staging multiple houses in the near future. If your goal is to create a unique house, renting the furniture is the best option.

There will be certain costs, but they are not mandatory in the event that they are to store the furniture between times of no use. A provision must be included within your budget.

When buying furniture, it's acceptable to compromise on the quality, as it's the design that is important here.

Aesthetics: Keeping furniture design simple and neutral can help. Choose simple lines and neutral colors that can be adorned by a variety of affordable accessories that can be used in many houses. You can search for furniture from a variety of sources including online shops or second-hand dealers (here make sure the furniture isn't or damaged) and local furniture stores, and even your own or mom's basement.

The house can be decorated with only the smallest of decoration, but make sure that there's art above the seating area an arrangement of fresh flowers placed on the table to the side, a cushions for accents or anything that evokes warmth and warmth inside the house. Make sure the drapes are open so that plenty of sunlight can enter the home, bringing more life and vibrancy. In this regard it must be remembered that no room within the home should contain any photos of personal belongings. These personal possessions should be removed since the goal is for the prospective buyer to envision the house as his home, and the items could be distracting for the buyer.

Logistics: When you have completed the stage your house is finished the house, you must choose the right storage for all the items that you've bought, as well as the best method to move it into and out of homes. In this situation the most obvious option is to engage movers and it is the most effective option as you will be able to ensure that your furniture is transported to storage in a professional way.

For storage, it is best to locate the most affordable storage space that is also the most secure regardless of how difficult you find it or the distance is. One alternative is to keep your stuff within the garage. Another option is to store it in in an indoor space on the lower floor. It is best to pay a bit more for a climate-controlled unit, so that your wood furniture is kept without being impacted by extreme weather conditions.

The home must appeal to potential buyers and staging is one method to do this. Mind you, it will result in positive results.

Chapter 12: Aesthetic Update

Option

Strategies for flipping are crucial to be successful in business world, and there are some that are simpler to implement than other strategies. Certain strategies are only for experienced individuals, such as those who have gone through the first two books of this series. People who know the process of flipping houses and want to make a difference to their life quality and who are looking to become more knowledgeable about the topic.

The other strategy that may be useful for those seeking to flip homes to make money is the basic aesthetic enhancement option. Most people do not have the expertise required to complete significant home improvements, such as renovating a bathroom, but without the assistance of a knowledgeable person, such as contractors. Contractors cost a lot of money however they are expensive, and investing the money in excess could make a huge difference to the potential profit. This is why it may occasionally be beneficial to invest in areas without any intention of improving.

Aesthetic Update

The way to achieve this is to use your lack of expertise for your benefit. You might not be knowledgeable about fixing light fixtures or other upgrades which could be pertinent to selling the home that you purchased for a greater value However, that doesn't mean that you are unable to sell houses.

In the beginning, you must find houses on the market that is sold low prices. As was mentioned previously there are certain characteristics to look out for when looking for the best deal. Foreclosures and similar offers an opportunity to make an income from the real estate investment. The majority of houses are listed at a price that is below market value as a result of issues they face such as a bad appearance or other. So, if you come across the house you want to buy that doesn't require major repairs that you do not have the expertise and skills to complete then you can buy it to be flipped.

Instead of waiting for months to revamp and enhance the overall appearance of the place it is possible to make it appear as if you have made improvements. When you buy the "fixer upper" location that is offered for sale at a price that is far lower than the most desirable homes on the market it can give the impression that the house is in better condition than it was prior to. Making only minor changes to the exterior of the property and the appearance, you can boost the market value.

Spend a couple of weeks to make these small changes. Make sure to plant a few flowers and mow the lawn and paint the front door. If you do these three simple items, you will dramatically transform the look of the home. It will become less of an eye-sore and more of a beneficial addition to the neighborhood. It not only increases the value you get for it however, it also increases the value of the houses around it. The capability to boost the market is quite accessible through following the steps for this particular method.

One of the most common mistakes people are prone to make when they try to make money from the method of aesthetics-based flipping houses is to charge excessively for their home after making these tiny adjustments. Although some may be impressed, nobody would believe that the house has been completely revamped. It is important to ensure that you earn profits, however you must do more than just make ends meet. It isn't easy to accomplish this particularly if you're not sure how to go about it.

The most effective method to determine the right price to offer is to take the average of all the surrounding home prices. To determine the average of something, combine all of the possible numbers--mostly within a single block. Then, you must divide the sum by the total of numbers. In other words, if there's 10 houses in the block and three are worth 100 thousand dollars, two are 110 thousand dollars and five are 145 million dollars, then you'd add all the numbers, then divide the total by 10. The sum of the numbers will be the mean price of the homes within the neighborhood.

The mean of that set is $124,500. If you pay less than the price for the home--which is what you must have done in order to make money since you took into consideration the entire cost upfront as this book teaches you to do, you should be able to earn profits. This won't be as significant of a difference however, because it involves less effort, it's technically a higher return. It is also possible to complete multiple jobs in a lesser amount of time, which can result in an increase in profits as well.

The option of aesthetics is a fantastic method to earn a little bit of cash without putting any risk like traditional home flipping. This allows you to earn money while avoiding the risk.

Chapter 13: Tax On House Flipping Consequences

House flipping is very popular when real estate is rising in value. House flippers purchase properties and sell them to make a profits. In certain regions where property values have dropped and investors have suffered huge losses. However, the new house flippers shouldn't be discouraged. Flipping houses can be an investment that is profitable in the event that the home flipper is aware of the risks and works to avoid these.

Many investors believe that flipping houses is more profitable than trading in stocks because real estate is tangible. You can view the house as well as the neighborhood. They are able to easily determine if the property is an excellent choice for investment, or not. If they're reckless in their earning it is possible that the Internal Revenue Service may receive an increased portion of the earnings. Many home flippers continue with their plans without taking into consideration the tax implications. In reality, a majority of them don't know about taxation.

The majority of investors believe that they can purchase a home and renovate it, then sell it to make a profits. They think that the rollover provision to benefit them. The rollover provisions permitted homeowners to utilize the funds they made from the sale of their home to purchase a more expensive home. But, as of 1997 these rules no longer existed. In the present the homeowner who sells his primary residence may get an exemption from tax if he resided in the house for a long period of time. However, if the property was an investment it isn't eligible for tax breaks. apply.

In addition, many of investors believe in this assumption that they could easily make a fortune by flipping houses. But, in their rush to make cash, they don't recognize that taxes could greatly cut their profits. They must realize that they could reap greater benefits if taking the time to do it slowly.

Tax on capital gains is assessed on all investment earnings. In general, tax rates are based according to the time that the property has been owned prior to selling it. When the house is held less than 1 year, then the gains are taxed in the ordinary income. However, if the property is kept for longer and the capital gains tax could be as small as 15 percent. Some house flippers are not willing to hold the property for at least one year. Therefore, they have to have to pay up to 35% tax on income from the property.

The Internal Revenue Service considers short-time real estate transactions to be an entity, especially in the event that there are many of them in the course of a year or more. Thus, those who flip houses will be assessed regular income tax on real property transactions. The IRS scrutinizes every transaction carefully to determine if the appropriate amount of tax is paid. If a person who flips houses is assessed normal income tax for the real estate transactions because the IRS discovered that the property is an enterprise, the owner will be assessed an additional self-employment tax , which is currently 15.3 percent.

Chapter 14: Property Criteria

Comfortable Underground Sales

Price

The most natural way to go about buying a flip is to examine the most competitive price. "Oh this property is selling for $800,000 and the house is just 500 square feet, therefore it's likely to fetch the sum of $795,000!"

The issue is that you have to be prepared for the worst-case scenario. Are there comparables to the house worth $800,000 that recently sold for $500,000? After further investigation does it appear to be identical to the theme?

Yes I'm sure that your flips appear better than the ones sold at $550,000! You might be told, "There is nothing even like it!" In any case, the $ 550,000 Comp provides a reasonable market value to flip. I'm not saying that it'll be sold for $550,000 If it doesn't go as planned, ensure that the house is sold at least the amount.

This doesn't necessarily mean that it's a deal breaker, but it is when you purchase the house for $300,000 or so. To build or get the deal to work it is necessary to sell anything worth more than $550,000. It could succeed however, in the event of a disaster I'm sure the transaction will earn an amount of $ 550,000.

"POP" POTENTIAL

Now that the comfortable basement numbers are in place, we can see if there's the possibility of a significant upside. (Note There's the reason that a comfy underground sales price is prior to this.)

The $800,000 price is certainly a good price for the property you want to purchase. Better yet, you can have two couples who are that are in the $ 700,000 to $ 800,000 range. After talking to some smart realtors, they made a decision about how highest selling prices were brought.

In many instances they are located in low well-stocked areas. Homes are sold at a price that is below market, buyers arrive the prices of hundreds of thousands more than other properties. It is true that it is an actual comp however, it's an individual buyer. This is typically the scenario for Silicon Valley, where I flip, which makes it difficult to underwrite.

This is why it is vital to know an eventual "pop" turn story. Was it listed for sale at $ 775,000, then put up for sale in two weeks, then sold at $800,000? I believe this is a much superior offer than the house initially listed at $600,000.

If you decide to sell two houses in the 700-$150,000 range the sale will look excellent and could assist in raising the "comfortable cost of selling underground."

Near the MEDIAN PRICE of a REGION or CITY

Are you planning to build the most beautiful and largest home I've seen in this area What do you think? If so, then, at the very least it is more likely to make a loss.

How many people are able to afford the most luxurious and costly homes in the region? Perhaps. But what if they're not on the market for homes or simply do not want to use them too much? Your flip is able to sit down.

It's as if you're playing with an unsound recorder, however this isn't a huge issue as the market is booming in the current situation. But, issues can occur when things begin to cool.

The answer is to look for properties that are being resold at rates that are similar to the median cost for the area or city. How many buyers are at the moment?

The idea is to search at a market that has an abundance of potential buyers. If your property is excellent, it is likely to be in some sort of bidding battle.

CLARIFY THE VALUE STORY WITH ADDED VALUE

The first question you should ask an agent before giving a flip to the agents would be "What is the background of the property?" In reality, what I really want to find is an indication of suffering. "The house was passed down through the generations however no one had been there for many years and there was a significant damages to the roofing.

They required money and planned to sell the house immediately." This is a great story as it teaches you how to increase value and the reason why a home is being sold at a lower price.

The most important thing is to understand how you can increase the value of a property to generate profits through flips. It could be the capacity to sell quickly and cash, or to undertake a massive refurbishment or even add-on/rebuild scenarios. Each of these options has restrictions that hinder entry, and also explain how you are able to trade over these.

It's prudent to avoid purchasing a home that appears to be for sale at a fair price. Don't get me wrong. I'm sure it's fine to purchase a house for the best price, but I'd like to make clear why I'm getting an excellent deal. With the advancement of technology for real estate and the rise of technology, everyone should be contemplating what their house will be worth (perhaps even an overinflated notion). I am more confident about buying an apartment if I am able to show myself how I could make money.

NORMAL LAYOUT

This is among the most ignored elements of a prospective flipper home. The layout is crucial. I'm working with several houses built in the 1950s, with some wacky additions. The old saying "pig lipstick" could be a loss.

More embarrassing is the fact the fact that there's no simple solution for Winchester Mansion. A roof that is leaky is not ideal but at least , there's a reasonable cost to fix it. A home with a poor layout is, naturally irreparable unless you damage the entire structure.

I'm aware that the term "normal arrangement" is a subjective term and somewhat ambiguous. The test you can use while wandering around your house is to determine if you can envision the floor layout. It's not difficult, but the layout is comfortable. Another method to utilize is to use women as every man in the room since they know these things more than the majority of males.

NICE SURFORROWING HOUSING

Are you purchasing the most impressive home on the block, or is it one of the worst? The other houses in the neighborhood aren't required to be renovated However, a little bit of personal control can make a difference. Also be wary of houses that look ugly or have a problem with their owners.

Take a walk through the neighborhood at various hours of the day, and chat with people in the street. It might be awkward, but if you are truthful, tell me what you're doing today. The majority of people are willing to be a part of the dirt in their community.

What is the 70 percent rule?

"The rule of 70 percent" says that an investor must take 70 percent on the value of the property, minus repairs required. This is known as the post repaired value , and it is the amount an individual home's value is after repairs are completed.

Chapter 15: Funds In Flipping

There's a quote for investors that "it is necessary to earn money". Prior to making the decision to venture into flipping, be aware of the fundamentals that every home flipping business begins with the search for a property that you can flip. Once you've identified a property, you must money to purchase the property. This is only the beginning. In addition, there is charges for the holding of the home (which include insurance and HOA fees, as well as other costs associated with owning a home) in the event that it is needed to make a renovation the materials will be bought for the purpose of renovation. In order to finish it off the realtor's cost along with the agent's cost and closing costs which will require additional funds. Thus, flipping is all focused on money and money. The more you invest, the more you can are expecting to receive in return. You can choose to invest as there are a variety of methods to find money to start the fix-and-flip business that lets you purchase your property, and then do the things needed, and then sell it out, make a return on your investment and pay your allotted amount. It's not as simple as it sounds.

There are many ways flippers can obtain funds to work with , however after the recession that took place in 2008/2009 the process for funding has become more complicated and time-consuming and you must demonstrate a creative and innovative ability to obtain the results you desire.

You must be educated and understand the financing patterns that will benefit you prior to making a decision to apply for an loan. If you are armed with a bit of knowledge about these topics, you can speed up the borrowing process:

4.1 Create a Business Plan for Every Flip

When flipping houses, you have to repair homes that aren't in good state. In the event of loaning money, you should calculate the amount needed to complete your plan. The business plan will be presented to the lender in connection with the loan you're seeking. The business plan's booklet isn't required to be huge It just needs to be thorough and well-organized.

Your essay should comprise of the following elements:

Property address

The cost of housing in the world

Budget plan, timeline and the financial cost of renovation

Business partner and background details

Plan B in the event that the renovation does not go according to plan.

4.2 What is the cost of Renovating

To ensure that you do not borrow less than what is needed, which could significantly impact your project You must create an elaborate and thorough plan of action before deciding on the amount that you're seeking. There should be a plan of the different repairs to be done to the property you plan to turn. The scope of work you choose to undertake is crucial to accomplish this task. It's not enough to just sit and create your own scope of work. you require the assistance of experts such as appraisers and contractors who are experienced. They will examine the property and estimate the costs of the materials that will be needed to bring the property in good condition including the costs of labor. Its scope should also include loan-to value (LTV) as well as after-repair value (ARV). The LTV involves comparing the amount of the loan with the worth that the house is worth. The most effective LTV value is approximately 90 percent. ARV is the estimation of the worth of the home after repairs are completed.

4.3 Take Your Tentacles

Your connection in real estate determines how far you go. A strong financial connection is crucial to obtain money. For investors who aren't familiar, it can be difficult to convince people to be able to trust them with their money Therefore, to simplify things you should become a member of with your Local Real Estate Investors Associations (REIA) to network with investors from other areas and become connected. The most successful and experienced real estate investors perform both. They apply for loans to finance their investments and then provide loans to individuals' projects. Therefore, you shouldn't underestimate the value of the local investors.

These are the places where you can find the money you need to start your flipping business.

4.4 Lending by Family and Friends

We've emphasized the importance of connections when it comes to investing in real estate. If you've got a one-on-one relationship with people, wonderful possibilities are in store when you flip your business. Friends or relatives might one day become your flip lender since you have a strong and reliable relationship with them. Sometimes they may introduce you to individuals who are willing to contribute to your project. There are people who have an interest in investing in property, but don't possess the necessary time nor the knowledge to manage the team and, as such, would happily invest in your project. Because you are directly connected to your lender, you can be sure that the interest rate you pay is low and cost-effective.

There are certain aspects to take into consideration and implement when borrowing money from relatives and friends. The first is to make sure you write the terms and conditions of any loan in writing so as to prevent future disputes and maintain a cordial relationship between all. The agreement books the interest rate as well as payback period must be documented and strictly adhered to. Additionally the entire IRS or security regulations must be applied to the family loan and friend loan. Thirdly, inform the lender know that investment funds work and that he can be prepared to pay the loan until the property is closed.

4.5 Private Investorsor Hard Money

Cash in the bank! It sounds scary. You should examine the portion that is described in the form of private investors. Hard money is money obtained by private investors. These are loans that cannot be taken out by banks, but are obtained through private investment. Certain wealthy individuals may want to invest in real estate developments but aren't able to be on their own or perform the necessary work in real estate Therefore, they opt for the possibility of lending cash to those who are interested. It is less stringent requirements to be able to obtain unlike bank loans, and is able to be received within two weeks. The money you can get through hard cash can be obtained from family and friends of relatives who want to invest in real estate ventures but aren't able to commit the time and knowledge required for the business. The ability to borrow money by means of hard money is costly and scarce alternative, and you'll get lucky if you've got wealthy relatives or friends who are willing to invest. The project should be evaluated with a professional real estate lawyer who is aware of every term and conditions and will explain the details to you, and the implications should you not be able to complete the project within the time specified. Make sure you are aware of the rates for interest as well as the way to pay and the consequences in the event of a project failing before taking the plunge into lending with hard money.

4.6 Find a Finance Partner

This method of financing is ideal for those who are skilled in flipping houses and have an in-depth understanding of how to find the perfect financial partner. An investor in the flipping business doesn't just contribute his portion of the cash but also assists in making the flip successful. Finance partners can be involved in the search for the right property to flip or manage, as well as the preparation and planning of the property's improvement and then the most important factor (finance). In the majority of cases the amount of profit is contingent on the contribution of each partner to the project , or they could reach a compromise over how profits are divided. In some instances one partner will take the responsibility for the fund, while the other searches for opportunities to flip. The decision of whether to choose only one partner or switch partners for every project is your own. Similar to what you do with family and friends, any agreement and the terms of it should be properly documented.

4.7 Personal Credit

However, personal loans could cause a decline in your credit score, but it provides you with the option of a payment plan that is predictable , in addition to loans with an interest rate that is fixed. Personal loans are appropriate for those with excellent credit and require only just a little amount of cash. If you believe that your credit card and your personal earnings are excessive it is possible to take out personal loans that you can be used to fund your flipping project. The majority of lenders require that your credit card to have a credit score of the 620 mark to make sure you'll be able to pay back the loan. Personal loans are an extremely flexible method of financing.

4.8 Credit Cards

The credit card is a suitable option when seeking funds. They have the distinct advantage of being quick, reliable and flexible. It's cost-effective when used it comes to short-term loans, but could yield rates of up bis 21%, or more in the long term. The possibility of making use of a credit card to fund real estate investment requires some creativity and some scientific research. It's a good idea and more comfortable when you have a good credit score and an income that can ensure it. There are a variety of methods of operating credit cards, as described below.

Cash advance: certain credit cards are made to give you access to an advance cash option that comes with more interest when as compared to purchase. Additionally, you could be eligible to pay a cash advance charge that is 2.

Balance transfer: many are in agreement on a low-rate balance transfer. You can make use of one to pay off the debts you've paid.

Materials: Some credit cards are used to purchase the equipment needed for the job. If you're able to buy the final item on the credit line, then you will be able to boost the cash flow of your business by obtaining credit card usage that is interest-free for a period of between two and three months.

4.9 Mortgage Financing

It might be challenging to secure a traditional loan to purchase properties, however, nevertheless there is no need to lie to lenders about the intentions you have for the property you wish to purchase. There are instances when you purchase properties and then decide to remain in the property for a time before selling it, so ensure that all intentions you have for any property you'd like to purchase be known to lenders in order to avoid being asked being asked questions. There are two kinds of mortgage financing that investors can use to their advantage. They are:

Cash-out refinances: When you do the cash-out refinance, you can make use of more than the current balance of your mortgage to refinance the property. There's always an additional fund , which is the one after loan expenses, that you are able to spend however you want.

Home Equity Loan: Also known as a second mortgage, it is a kind of debt that lets you spend your money on whatever you want to. You only make interest payments on the money you used. It is described as the money you get from the equity you have in the property you own. This amount determined by a comparison between the current market value and the mortgage balance of the investor. The home equity loan or your equity stake in the property is your collateral to the lender. The amount to which an investor is permitted access to is according to a combined loan-to value ratio (CLTV) that is between 80-90 percent of the worth for the house. The traditional home equity loan comes with conditions for repayment that comprise a fixed amount, including interest. To be eligible for a home equity loan you need to have credit that is reasonable and a steady monthly income that will allow you to pay off your mortgage as well as the mortgage and the home equity loans.

4.10 Financing

This is ideal for people who have the money to begin their journey or have retirement savings. However, it's not suitable for those who are getting close to or nearing retirement. You may decide to get an advance loan or cash out of the funds in your 401(k) accounts. The younger people who have just started saving may choose to utilize this method if they feel the security of benefits is greater than the risk. With this method, you're almost taking out an outright loan and then paying interest along with the money. and the most interesting part is both your loan as well as the interest are returned to your bank account, so the funds are yours.

4.11 Funds from seller

It is also known by the term owner finance. In this case, the owner of the property is also acting as the loanee. This is often difficult because homeowners generally want the cash immediately, and some traded it in exchange for the cash they earned from the proceeds. In the event that the vendor is looking to finance it, then it's beneficial. Seller lending can be very beneficial to both the seller as well as the buyer. The seller sets a deadline (balloon date) when the buyer is required to repay the loan. The investors may not completed the project, and therefore the buyer must repay the loan on his own or find other loans. Like every loan, all agreements should be written. It is also suggested that you engage a lawyer in the process of drafting and keeping the loan documents.

4.12 Business Line of Credit

If you've been involved in flipping for a long time and have a good track record of success and you are able to be able to access banks financing. The business credit line is better alternative to a conventional bank loan for real estate investors who are flipping. This kind of loan entitles you to a set amount of cash, but you only pay for the amount utilized. This makes the commercial line of credit the most suitable choice for those who aren't sure about the amount you will spend on renovations and renovations. Also it has an interest cost that is low , but you are able to be eligible to get it having credit that is good. Business lines of credit functions similar to the equity home in operation, however, it is distinct in the amount of amount of money you're exposed to. You can request a commercial line credit from your local bank, or a small business credit lines at Bank of America, Chase, Fargo, and Wells.

Chapter 16: Unimaginable Value Of Immovable Property

"Real estate cannot be taken or lost. If it is purchased using common sense and paid in full and handled with the utmost care, it's among the most secure investments anywhere in the world."

- Franklin D. Roosevelt

A Sneak Peep at the Prospects

For those of you who are lucky the younger generation of adults are eyeing other riches, like experiences! If you've not noticed it but by scouring your feeds on social media, you'll see that the majority of younger people, and even quite some who are part of Generation X prior to them are more interested in aspects like traveling and experiencing. Therefore, the market for immovable properties has been at an extent to a halt as they took over most part of our workforce.

At the time the world was more simple and the individual's desires and goals were more traditional, leading individuals to take financial choices that were more geared towards domestication. That's the reason why baby boomers – probably your parents - could proclaim the safety of owning a home at the end of their 20's and in their early 30's. Today, however, our minds tend to focus on less long-lasting "investments."

According to research that millennials aren't as inclined or willing to buy properties due to their desire to explore the world and invest money on traveling. Fashion, technology and high-end items are second on the list of millennials' things they need, so living with dad and mom for a few years isn't the best option for cutting expenses.

It's also interesting that younger couples are getting married much later than their counterparts in the boomer generation. With a growing number of young people reaching the wedding age to their mid-30's and the need to purchase homes doesn't attract the interest of these young people until they've made the decision to get married to their partner later on in their lives.

Why would any of this benefit you, you humble homeowner? According to the statistics the market for real estate is expected to increase by 5 years when all the millennials decide it's the right time to start making real investment.

Between now and when the property market has reached a record post-recession low as a result of the growing trend of renting instead of purchasing.

This means for you, it means that there are more options and less competition in the search for possible investments.

There's even more potential for those who dare to sell their homes. Experts predict that the millennial generation will soon recognize the need to invest in property as well as that an increase in demand will be seen in the next five to 10 years as they realize the benefits of owning a home and have the financial capacity to purchase their own house. At this point at this point, it's an inch ahead of the rest.

Why not start a business?

The most difficult decision for people who have a burning desire to earn more money is whether to create the business of their choice or invest in real property. There is no doubt that both options come with their own pros and cons. And for each person who has decided to flip houses there's probably thousands of others who have decided to go into the business world.

Why might it not be the right choice for you? Think about the negatives.

They're fickle

In contrast to homes - that are essential all year long, businesses are more likely to be impacted by seasons. For instance, ice-cream stores have more customers times of summer, but only a few customers during colder weather. That means you'll need to account for the off-season to offset your costs while it's sunny.

The issue? It isn't always identical. Therefore, while you might be able establish a sort of pattern over two years, the situation could shift in your third year. This is especially the case when a rival with hyped up offerings and more facilities opens right next to you, which could completely alter your projections in the end.

Finding a niche can be difficult.

It's not enough to decide on the business you want to start and then be completed with it. Many business owners realize that it's essential to conduct study to find the market gaps. It's sometimes not the gaps however, but the market's preferences. What are the things that patrons would like to be able to see? What are their preferences?

If you decide to take the route, you'll realize that there's an array of aspects you might not have even considered when the thought of running a business first popped into your mind. It's about the size of your business as well as the particular items and services that you have to provide, as well as what you could do to improve your business structure to distinguish yourself from your other businesses.

In addition it is important to know your target market. Who would like to purchase your product? Do you have a customer who needs your service? What is their age and where do they reside and what are the best ways to help them attempt to find an organization similar to yours?

Understanding your audience in depth is an essential element of knowing how you can create your own brand. Also belief that you can pick whatever you want when it comes to starting a business may be a complete sham because it's all about satisfying customers.

What happens if you make an incorrect market? That's why companies fail. It's a shame.

They're costly and time-consuming

Perhaps the most challenging aspect of running a business and one that many hopefuls overlook is that they consume quite a lot of time and cash. Much like a new baby, a brand new business idea requires the majority of, if not all of your time and energy. You must be attentive to every step of the process because success relies on it.

Apart from taking up a huge part of your daytime hours business also requires lots of green. The less cash you can spare more unattractive your business's beginnings may be to potential customers. Of course, you'll be able to grow later when you earn a few dollars however don't expect to make any in the near future.

The reality of running the business you are in is that, for the first few months, you won't earn a profit. It's a harsh reality, but it's true however. It may take some time to get your business picked up. In the initial few months following the time you allow your small venture to stand on its own two feet, you'll need to make the right moves to attract customers.

So, who pays the electricity, the salary and benefits of employees and loan amortization for furniture and equipment you may have bought or rented, as well as other expenses associated with overhead? Of course, you do. The longer you take to turn a profit the more likely you'll be paying for everything from your pockets.

Sure, when the flow of cash begins to improve then you don't have to reach into your pockets any more isn't it? It's not true. Certain months may see higher in sales than the other, but some months may have negative figures.

Therefore, the majority of the profits you earn should be reserved for rainy days. If you're anticipating a down increase in cash-in the next month, any profits you earn today ought be put aside to pay for your overhead the following month.

It's a challenging and frequently difficult balance, and if you don't have the time to do it, your business can be extremely vulnerable to loss.

What investment?

Some people believe that purchasing equipment for their business is considered to be an investment, however one of the most fundamental elements of of an investment is its transferability. It should be versatile and adaptable. It must have a vital worth even in the setting of a market.

If there aren't any other reasons to use that 6-station rotary screen printer other than making prints, then it's certainly not an investment. If your business is going downhill and you decide to sell, then you're probably not likely to be in a position to sell the screen printing equipment at its full price, leading you to suffer losses.

If you are a business owner the only real investment that you can make to consider is the brand. Brands that are successful become franchise-worthy, which basically means that people will spend money to own an independent branch of your company. The business model you offer and they pay for the cost of capital and overheads, and you receive the profits from the sales.

What are the companies that provide franchising? McDonald's, 7/Eleven, and Subway for instance. Which of them have they in common? They're all famous. In the case of hopefuls, it may be years or even a lifetime to gain the same level of fame.

If you've had a good run in the last few years, if your business isn't sufficiently established to market franchises, the only way to earn more profit off of your name would be to transfer it to a different company completely. This would mean giving up your ownership rights and forfeiting any rights to the company you put your heart into.

Why not build and sell?

Then, why do you flip? Why not simply purchase land, construct something stunning on it, and then sell it instead? Sure, it's more convenient to create something beautiful from the beginning instead of having to contend with the ugly, dreadful demons of a deteriorating mid-century home.

However There's plenty of profits to be made from homes that are in disrepair. For instance, foreclosures can be priced as high as 37 percent less than similar houses. Sure flipping a foreclosure could be a completely different undertaking in and of itself however, for the experienced real estate property professional it could be more lucrative because the initial cost of purchasing the property is low.

There are many additional reasons to think about buying old homes and flipping them at an income in contrast to making a house and then selling it.

They're generally less expensive

Based on the location in which you're operating in, you may discover that older homes can cost three or four times less than starting from scratch. For instance, you may discover a house that is worth $115,000 USD. You could add a few thousand dollars to add some charm and then flip it at $225,00 USD.

Instead of buying buildings and land, this is a less expensive threshold, allowing you to benefit from the advantages of investing in properties without having to pay an amount. What is the reason building costs are high?

Labor and the price of materials is at record highs and are not accessible to the majority of investors. This is especially true when you have nothing to start with, thus limiting the options available and potentially compromising the build quality of your home you build due to an insufficient amount of money.

They're quicker

It's not known as house "flipping" without a reason. The process of purchasing an existing house, transforming it, and then putting it back for sale in the space of a few months is lightning-fast, which can yield excellent returns. Many house flippers keep the properties they purchase for several months or up to a year.

Based on ATTOM Data Solutions, the average return by flipping during the 3rd Quarter of the year 2017 United States was $66,448. If this is all completed within the space of six months, you could earn more than $130,000 USD in a single year.

This is assuming you're flipping one home at each time.

If you build and sell you could wait for longer than a year before you are able to present your business to the attention of the public. The lengthy process of obtaining permits for construction, as well as the inevitable construction delays that you may not get the same amount of money when you build from scratch.

They can be more profitable

There are many elements that affect the profit potential of flipping a home. Location, timing as well as competition, quality of construction and interest rates, demand and yes, even the past of the house you've picked could all have an enormous influence on the amount of profits you'll earn off of it.

However anyone who is able to do things right could earn an extremely lucrative gain. In fact, the flipper could earn more than constructing or selling a brand new house.

Naturally, things do be unpredictable, and situations are never the same. However, generally speaking, the majority of people who are interested in investing and investors who are successful in particular - tend to lean toward flipping more instead of building and selling due to the fact that it's significantly more profitable, even after one or two years.

Are There Any Risks?

There isn't anything like a perfect investment or business venture. It is important to realize that there will be risks that may arise from your own errors or what you do with the business itself. In that case, you may be wondering - what's the problem when you flip houses?

Flip Might Flop Flip Might Flop

There are many home flipping horror stories about investors who fail to earn a profits within the right timeframe. With such a volatile market it is difficult to find a way to know if you'll be able to achieve the sale, even if you've taken all the proper steps.

If you aren't able to sell the property soon after the renovations are completed and if you weren't able to purchase the property in full, you'll have to pay the mortgage out of your own pockets until it is able to attract the interest of a reliable buyer. This - also known as the holding cost an extremely risky situation that could be a nightmare for any investor. number of problems.

Property Unpredictability

It is common for flippers to look for possible investment opportunities in auctions and foreclosures. These auctions and foreclosures are where you can purchase a house at a very low cost which makes it a great option to secure a suitable property for a modest capital investment.

The drawback? buying through auctions means you don't get the chance to thoroughly inspect the home before you purchase. Although it may appear nice and well-built from a distance but a closer inspection could find significant flaws that could dramatically increase repair and renovation costs.

The foundations are faulty, as is mildew and mold, as well as the necessity for complete repair and restoration of plumbing could cause you to end up paying more for repairs than you'd earn after the sale.

Be prepared for the unexpected

It's a shame, but this is the one thing that flipping houses shares with entrepreneurship. While keeping up with the most current news about real estate will help you identify trends, the reality is that the market for real estate could change within just a few seconds.

In addition, the process of renovating are also prone to causing several frights. Being late to deadlines, not understanding the effort required to fully restore an old property, or enduring some glitches during the process could make you grin while you lose money over hours spent managing and reworking a home.

Why You Should Proceed Them All

It's true that you did not sign up to fail and nobody wants to take on the risk of losing their your hard-earned money on a venture that doesn't succeed. But be aware that success is likely if you ensure you're playing your cards well. Every investment or business possibility is accompanied by its own distinct set of risks and losses that could be incurred, but should you not take the plunge and test it out at the beginning you'll never have the chance to succeed.

If you're unsure if investing in real estate is the best option for you, take a look at some of the general benefits of purchasing real property in the first place:

Demand Will Always Be There

So, maybe you put your investment in the market at the wrong moment and it's sitting there, waiting to be bought by buyers who don't appear to be there.

Even though no real estate investor would like to waste time trying to be able to take a bite of advertising for homes, you need to keep in mind that houses will always be in high demand. No matter how bleak the market appears at any point in time it is certain that there will be buyers looking for homes because there are always those who require houses!

Give it a couple of years and the real estate market will increase and provide you with the opportunity to draw a crowd of buyers who are waiting to get first-dibs on your property. Of course, if discover that you'll be unable to sell when you've finished your renovations it's possible to turn to renting.

In the present day age where younger adults tend to be more involved in other costs, homes are pushed to the side. Therefore, any millennial will like to rent a space as it allows them to have more flexibility as well as less obligation. If you do decide to let your home out and you want to keep it, you can hold it at the expense of your mortgage monthly to offset the cost of the holding and help you stay within break-even.

Prices will continue to rise.

The trend we've observed each year gives property owners assurance that they've picked the best investment to put funds on. This is the constant, consistent growth in the value of homes over time. In the past decade the market for property across the United States has seen a steady increase in real estate prices and is expected to double in the next few years.

What means for flippers is that while there is a real chance that you won't be able to sell as quick as it takes from 6 months to one full year. However, there'll be the possibility that prices will increase as the years progress. If you don't sell it right now but you could sell it to a higher price tomorrow, so you're able to reduce the loss.

It's as real as it gets!

The primary benefit in real estate lies in the fact that it's is it real! It's not a thing you can alter and it isn't a subject to theft It doesn't shrink with time, it doesn't die and is a constant. It's not like other investments such as cars that appreciate over the years, and gold, which is vulnerable to loss or theft, permanent properties are secure, and you are guaranteed that what you have today is what you'll be able to enjoy today.

The tides could change and the seasons could change and you may not be able to liquidate your investment when you'd like. However, as long as you have your name on the title, you'll be an extremely solid, uncorruptible investment that will add a substantial amount to your wealth.

Chapter 17: Final Thoughts

Congratulations! You're ready to head out and begin flipping houses. However, before you do that take a look at some important things to keep in mind before you embark on your journey to real property.

Get yourself educated

If you're reading this book, it's likely because you've not ever flipped a house. It's likely that you are not an agent licensed by the real estate industry. You're just dipping your feet in the waters. Don't enter the business without knowing what you are doing! You've already completed the first step to becoming educated through this book, but there's more to discover. Find more books, an mentor, collaborate with someone who is experienced, attend classes, and attend workshops both online or in-person. You may want to think about applying for a real estate permit if it is something you are planning to make a career of. In the end, it can save you lots in time as well as money.

Network

You're trying to create as large and solid of an online network as is possible. Like I said earlier, you need to locate someone to mentor you. The person you choose could be your partner in the first turn. This is the person you will be the most knowledgeable about and collaborate with the most.

Meet flippers! With social networks and Google meeting others on the internet and in person can aid you in your growth and development. Meet with veteran flippers and people who are novice to the sport as you. It is impossible to know how you could be able to aid each other on your make your way through your first adventure.

Joining a real estate group is extremely beneficial in many ways. In addition to making numerous contacts in business, but it can be a great option to create an

LLC or joint venture to aid in financing your business. There are many people who enter the business with zero money, and working together is often the best method to achieve your goals.

Make Your A-Team

I can't stress enough how important it is to have a competent team of professionals who will work with you from beginning to the end. If you believe that not having any professional from you team would be smart method to save money but you're making yourself vulnerable to failing. Look around, conduct your research, read reviews and find the top contractors, CPA, real estate agent, and other experts that you could require to help make your experience as efficient and as successful as it can be.

Market market!

Market is such an important term in the real estate business that I thought it was a good idea to review it once. The flip you plan to make will revolve around your market of choice, so it is crucial to learn the most information feasible. You'll select your market of choice when you purchase your home and, from there on, you'll be promoting, renovating and selling your home keeping in mind the market. Conduct as much study as possible in order to make the right decisions that will result in your success.

It is possible to be bad, but it can also be good.

Do not ignore your options in "bad" areas. While you'd like for your very first home flip the most straightforward one there is a good amount of money that could be made from these homes. Older homes and houses that have been abandoned can become gold mines. Take a look before you let them go. Are new businesses opening businesses in the region? What are the anticipated increase in population and income over the next couple of years? Generation Y is becoming the dominant buyers' market and are often looking for houses in these locations to cut costs. The good thing is that homes located in "bad" locations are usually very affordable and can be sold for an amazing profits.

There's more than one way to do it.

Take a look at your options to sell. Land contracts, wholesaling and leasing could earn an impressive profits. Take a look at every property carefully and think about the ways you could be able to make it gold by using any of the methods. You'll soon be adept at identifying profitable flips and the best ways to utilize them.

And last , but certainly not the least...

Don't hesitate!

I'm sure this info may seem overwhelming and somewhat overwhelming. Don't let fear stop you from making a move! If you are able to get through the first house , the toughest part will be gone. So long as you've learned and prepared yourself as best you can, you'll be successful. No matter if you make an income of $500 or $50,000 from your first home You have achieved success. Keep your eyes on the prize, be diligent, and never ever stop studying.

This is the story of a home flipper who started house flipping without even having a clue about what it was, but who in the end earned hundreds of thousands through careful planning and a meticulous budget.

Confessions of a frequent house flipper; a case study

"In 1996, in those days with Butcher Block Formica countertops, I began building custom homes. Between 1997 and 2007 I also purchased renovated and then turned over homes. This is now known as House Flipping, a term that became popular due to its appearance in cable television shows that focus on home renovations and rehabs. I was a brand new "Home Building and Renovation". In the present I like the idea behind that title.

In the early part of 1997, as I was working on the design and construction of various new houses I was driving through one of the neighborhoods in a the well-known Chicago suburb. There was something that seemed odd and I decided to slow down trying to figure out the underlying messages my builders' intuitions told me.

I drove slowly along one street, then down another. Then I retraced my steps back to the starting point and started again.

It wasn't long until I realized that this was the perfect place to purchase renovations, buy and sell. The streets were better than average and had lots of streetlights. A well-lit street makes people living there and the children they have secure and safe. The lawns were well-maintained. There was not a single piece of litter to be seen. It was quiet and contained plenty of trees to give the feeling of security for those who resided there.

I thought that at the period, a lot or even all of the inhabitants were retired or empty nesters citizens. The houses were small for families of today, however I quickly discovered that schools within the district were high-rated. Based on my experiences I was aware that large houses with tiny lots typically resulted in low taxes. Within a couple of days, I verified this with the building of our county.

Most importantly, there were many homes for auction. There are usually good reasons however in this instance it was simply people who were moving into condosor who were selling parents' house or estate. So, I came up with an idea.

I knocked at the door to one of the houses available, a small brick two-bedroom home, dating to the 1950's house on a large lot. There was no response on a weekday afternoon. So I left my card with an inscription on the back of the card that read I can find you buyers and make much more cash for your home'. The next evening, of course the couple in their mid-forties who resided in the house, called me. I explained that I was unable to discuss this on telephone, however I I would like to have the chance to speak about the matter in-person. The next Saturday we had a meeting and spoke about the house in front. "I would like to take a look at it from top to bottom to plan and add a room for a larger kitchen and to add another floor. (It was a single-story). I will assess the cost of the improvements and will have a vibrant and unique sign which no one will be able to ignore. We will place a few brochures on the shelf to the sign that will include the estimated cost of the home after the renovations are completed. You'll agree to sell the property to me when I have found a buyer for the price you have set and an extra 5-15% of profit above your asking price."

It took some time to be able to process all that information for us all! We parted ways but not before deciding to meet in the next week. I was sure that the decision was already taken. The next day I sketched an addition to the kitchen and an additional floor. The drawings were simple , but with a strong visual impact. They weren't meant for construction, but intended for marketing. On Monday morning, the couple called to ask if they would like to proceed to the next stage. I replied "Great!", though I wasn't aware of which step next would be. The next one, or the one following that. The day after, I gathered some details about the taxes and land and also learned regarding the schools in our area. They were far better than I expected.

On Friday I had a wealth of knowledge regarding the house, demographics of the neighborhood as well as the real estate market in our area and the banks that are in the vicinity. I conducted a line-by-line analysis of the rehab and the addition expenses. I confirmed my main expenses with my lawyer and my plumber, electrician, carpenter, and HVAC expert. I double-checked the price and set it less than a home similar to mine in a gentrified area of town. My estimates suggested that I could be able to achieve a 60k-75k profit. It felt like a good beginning, and on

Saturday, I had the opportunity to answer the question "What is the next step?

Before meeting with the owner I took a thorough tour of the garage and house. The most essential qualities were in good working order. the exterior bricks, the foundation as well as the framing plumbing, and the electric connection that ran to the building were in good working order.

Then we discussed. I shared the estimates that I was doing, and why I believed that the project could be a huge success. In terms of financials, we were in an excellent position. We neither the owners nor myself needed to invest any money prior to the time we found a buyer or buyers. In fact I would require construction funds once the new owner had fully committed. At that point, I would purchase the house from the previous owners at the predetermined price. They would hold off on their profits to accrue till the owners been able to close the property after the improvements had been completed.

Here's the 'Time Line"

Contract with the seller with all the necessary contingencies

Drawings that are complete for marketing and design a stunning signage and brochure

The buyer's contract with all the necessary contingencies

Apply for a permit, agree to agreements for trade, and make the work

Sign the purchase contract with the buyer

Then, you can finalize the arrangement for payment with the seller.

I am paying off my short-term loan and construction loan

You can deposit up to $75,000 in the bank

Get busy to cut down the capital gain tax liability

10. Buy the two houses that follow.

After the second Saturday meeting and check, everything seemed too amazing to be real. It is often stated in our industry that 'if it looks too amazing in fact, it likely is'. This time, however. I managed to get paid $ 65,000 for the work. These kinds of miracles can happen!

In addition, I purchased two additional projects, but I didn't wait until the tenth step. The third and second projects were signed prior to the first being completed. With a good cash flow plan I was able to make 20 percent down payment for the two homes that I was building. Everyone was content.

Conclusion

I hope that, after you've read this book, you will feel like you have the necessary information to begin flipping houses. There's a lot to be learned and you can gain a lot of knowledge through taking a trip out and performing. The method of flipping houses one that is possible for anyone who wants to be educated, to work hard and earn lots of money.

www.ingramcontent.com/pod-product-compliance
Lightning Source LLC
Chambersburg PA
CBHW071837080526
44589CB00012B/1029